T0354154

Prologue

Kenya HARA

In this book, I would like to approach our impression of "whiteness" through words. But this is not a book of history, and I make no claim to erudition. Instead, I propose to take a hundred "whites" from my collection of memories and write about them as they come to me, one by one, trying to relive each, entry by entry. I would like to do this until the description "white" merges with the air....

The four originary Japanese colors are red, blue, black, and white, or so it is said. These colors can be expressed as pure attributes. Red refers to that which flares up brightly like fire. Blue is the vision of a boundless expanse. Black is gloomy, bereft of all light. Whiteness is a radiance that stands out with utmost clarity against a chaotic background. Above all, I see "whiteness" as having a quality that transcends color. A designer's job is to make something emerge, to create a horizon of recognition that rises out of a cacophonous background. In other words, it is concerned with the conflict between figure and ground that occurs in the creation of an image. This "whiteness," or *itoshiroshi*, is what naturally draws our eyes towards a conspicuous image.

I formerly wrote that there is no such thing as white, only the sensibility that allows us to experience whiteness. If white is not a color, but a sensibility or mentality, then it is natural to approach white by collecting and arranging various white phenomena. As I write these pages, "whiteness" may gradually no longer appear white; I may no longer be able to describe it as white. But that shouldn't be a problem.

Unlike science, design does not place ultimate value on that which can be empirically demonstrated. The power of the designer's imagination is its drive to find what something may turn out to be. Design may be more like mathematics in that it aims to relearn through reason what the body—already a part of the physical universe—knows instinctively. And yet, the insights of design are not meant to be provable like mathematical theorems. A designer strives to notice something fresh and surprising within familiar phenomena: the appearance of water filling a cup to the brim, for example, or the painstakingly arrived at four tines of the fork or four legs of the chair, a single, carved book-printing type, or the whiteness and tautness of paper. A designer's work produces a sense of inspiration that leads us towards life and the universe. It should awaken hopes and ideals regarding both the way we live and our environments.

Although this book is written in words, I believe it is also a kind of act of design. I seek out whiteness in a variety of phenomena as though shelling nuts to reveal the meat inside, to touch their core. In a trance-like state, I use words to pull the shells away and examine the kernels within. Perhaps *100 Whites* is the resulting pile of shells.

I wrote each entry over the course of a single week, at a leisurely pace as though slowly pedaling a bicycle. Before I knew it, I had arrived at one hundred entries. Each day I would throw myself fully into the writing, feeling as though my senses were being bombarded on all sides. Thus, although the central idea and the style of the book may seem to waver or wander, the time I sat face to face with white was intensely focused, like hours spent at prayer. There were subjects that I knew I wanted to include no matter what, and as I approached the final entries, my own expectations began to weigh heavily on me. I decided I would allow the instinctive promptings of my heart to determine the form of the book, so the order of the entries has been left largely untouched. If you find yourself reading the entries in this book out of order, leafing through and stopping at what interests you most, that's all right with me. In fact, nothing would make me happier.

In *White*, which was published in 2008, I wrote that the "space" hidden in Japanese aesthetics, the state of emptiness, functions as a receptacle that can be filled with an infinite variety of meanings. I then discussed the exchange and circulation of such images. When we use the word "space," however, we inevitably approach the well-established notions of Taoism and Zen. Therefore, I couched my discussion of "white" in terms of space, that is "white" as a mediator, a conceptual key to exploring Japanese aesthetics.

After *White* was published, I continued to think about this until I realized that I now wanted to write about "white" as it relates to concrete phenomena rather than "white" as an idea. I wanted to explore in detail this strange theme that, unbeknownst to me, had been forming within my own sensibilities.

In Japanese, if you add one to white you get one hundred—that is, write a (一) over 白, and it forms 百. I found the courage to write this book by visualizing the *kanji* in this way. I wonder what you will see after passing through one hundred consecutive whites.

100 Whites

001 Bone

The character for *shiro*—白—is a visual representation of the various qualities of bone. It is a pictograph, it is said, etymologically linked with the image of a skull. In ancient China, where Japanese characters originated, wars between states were common. I expect there were many soldiers who fell in battle, and with no one to tend to them, they breathed their last in the depths of some remote wilderness. Exposed to the weather, their bodies were soon reduced to bones. Imagine you are walking across a field and, suddenly, there at your feet, is a human skull, that most fearful object, and other skeletal remains, bleached white by the sunlight. This "white" is nothing less than that horrifying presence appearing among the browns and greens of the wild.

Or, walking through the vastness of a desert, you catch sight of a pale glimmer against the brown sands—animal bones. Here is another striking illustration of life's elemental struggle. Coaxed by the wind, the dunes twist and turn like living creatures. They stretch to the horizon like never-ending waves while the wind carves subtle patterns into their surface. The bones are scattered across the smooth, rhythmic curves of the sweeping landscape—you see them against the jet-black shadows cast by the sun. Something changes. You realize you are confronting a harsh environment capable of snatching your life away.

For those sun-bleached bones, death is past. They no longer grieve the loss of life. Their attachments have vaporized, to rematerialize in some place far removed from the domain of the living. Scoured clean by wind and sand, whitened by the sun's ultraviolet rays, they are now nothing but death.

As if by some natural providence inaccessible to us, death has silently crystallized in the form of these bones. Their serenity is a distillation of the calm that awaits us on the other side. I imagine it was this contemplative feeling that the ancients expressed in the pictograph, "白." "White" is this crystallized death, but it is also "providence," "eternity," and even "beauty." Unlike the abstract concepts of sound-based language, these ideas are contained in a visual image. Land is said to be "green," and the planet is indeed filled with the myriad colors of rich organic life. Dark soil and lush, dense greenery convey life's energy, growth, and perpetual renewal. Within the context of such colors, white rises over life as death, stretching out to eternity.

When we utter "white" today, a trace of this mysterious significance is still present in the word. I believe that this subtle link to death persists because a record of its image was instilled in our first words and phrases, and in that form passed from generation to generation.

002 Milk

Milk white. A particular color, aroma, and texture, thick and opaque, immediately comes to mind. You recall that richness running down your throat. People are brought up on milk. We are, after all, mammals—we belong to the class of animals that suckle their young. In Japanese, the word *tarachine* means "parent"—literally, "hanging milk source." It suggests the pendulous breasts of a nursing mother, milk trickling from her nipples. This is our image of "milk white." We carry the impression with us, a common reference, or a *makura kotoba*, a poetic epithet or set form of words, that evokes a specific emotional response.

But why is milk the color it is? It is a question worth addressing. Whereas black absorbs all light, white reflects it. All wavelengths pass through something transparent. Depending on the length of its waves, we perceive light as the various colors of the rainbow. A tomato is red because it absorbs all other wavelengths and reflects only that wavelength people perceive as red. Milk appears white because its insoluble fats and protein particles diffuse all light's wavelengths. Of course, this is common scientific knowledge. Yet it doesn't provide an answer as to why milk is white or a tomato red.

Why does air appear transparent? The most satisfying answer is the theory that we, as living organisms, do not need to perceive it. If it were necessary for us to see air, a different form of vision would surely have evolved. If an ability to distinguish between types of air were an indispensable condition of life, if we had to avoid breathing harmful dark purple air or seek out safe, nutritious light-green air, we would have a corresponding form of perception. Our senses provide us with what we need. For example, we don't need to identify peril by scent, and so we have survived with a very limited sense of smell, barely able to sniff out gases.

Milk is a different matter. Without milk, babies would not survive. It was therefore essential that its appearance be plain and evident to us. That milk is white—that it diffusely reflects all wavelengths thanks to its fats and proteins—is thus a natural providence.

The smell of milk, too, is significant; it is associated with the warm security that emanates from a mother's body. Fresh milk smells good, but gradually turns sour as time passes, letting us know it has become dangerous to ingest. Milk's color, its smell, its viscosity, and its faintly sweet flavor are all signs of its value to us.

This brings to mind a scene from the novel *The Temple of the Golden Pavilion* by Mishima Yukio. In a reception room, a woman dressed in a beautiful kimono serves a cup of tea to a young army officer. He refuses to drink it. Finally, she opens the collar of her kimono, takes out one of her breasts, and squeezes some milk into the officer's teacup. Watching the scene from some distance, the novel's protagonist feels he can see the milk streaming from her breast as it foams in the green tea. The vivid whiteness of her powdered profile and her bare breast between the folds of her brilliant kimono…. Milk trickling down to froth in a cup of green matcha…. This is what we mean by *milk white*.

003   Paper

The essence of paper lies in the fact that it is easily dirtied and easily damaged. Indeed, paper's charm is its ephemeral nature; with its thinness and tautness it seems to be barely holding on to existence, and its tensile delicacy heightens our senses. Human wisdom, our ability to concentrate, our elaborate sensibilities, were all painstakingly acquired through our long confrontation with paper's purity.

"White" is most easily dirtied; "tautness" is most fragile. Paper historically influenced the development of our sense perceptions through its extremes of these two qualities. A fresh sheet of paper makes us sit up to attention with our backs nice and straight. We think of paper as delicate. Yet, we also sense that this delicacy is not confined to this or that sheet of paper. Rather, paper in general came to awaken those feelings within us that are delicate. This is the value and significance inherent in paper. Were it not for paper, humans might never have produced present-day culture in all its elaborate detail. We might not have come to possess our ability to concentrate, or to accumulate and store knowledge.

A "medium" provides a pathway for the creative will; it stimulates the desire to act, to go out and accomplish something. In this respect, paper has played an especially important role. In this era of electronic media, paper is now termed "print media." Of course, printing is still done with ink and the quality of paper plays an important role as well. Yet the phrase "print media" seems dismissive, unsubtle and unrefined. One could even say that this changed attitude is symptomatic of a certain naivete. In other words, perhaps the claims made for electronic media reveal a misunderstanding of paper.

The raw material for paper is a light-brown bark. This is pulverized into fine fibers and then soaked in water. When the resulting pulp is spread, pressed out on a plank, and dried in the sun it becomes paper—pure white and so taut that when held between two fingers you can stick a pin in it. Yet if you crumple it in your hand it can never again return to its original form. Paper thus represents the extremes of what is most vulnerable and most easily dirtied. How did we react when we first touched this most delicate material? We stained this fragile, pure white paper with deep black marks, folded, and even cut it. Actions that are both irrevocable and irreversible.

The thrill of making the first footprint on an unblemished field of snow. The instant in which that first sound is heard in a still, hushed concert hall. The moment a brush dipped in ink touches a sheet of pure white paper. Paper allows us to make a resolute leap towards the unexpected. A calligrapher's flicking brush, a poet's tentative word, a mathematician's flowing hypotheses. An author amasses revisions, a suitor writes a love letter, a typographer scrutinizes the beauty of letters before applying them to paper. There was a time when ceremony and decorum carried a weight, when a single piece of paper placed on a tray conveyed the depths of warm hospitality.

Paper is not just a means to archive information. It is one of humankind's most beautiful achievements. Our history is in part a history of being inspired, encouraged, and guided by paper. Paper awakens us.

004 Snow

> Taro is put to bed and the falling snow collects on his roof;
> Jiro is put to bed and the falling snow collects on his roof.

This is a poem by Miyoshi Tatsuji. Snow silently collects on a roof in the darkness of night. Evoked by this string of words is the image of quiet but thick-falling snow forming a lid over the world outdoors and out of sight. Perhaps this image derives partly from the way snow absorbs sound. I know that snow is not always welcomed by those who live in the snow country of Japan—they see so much of it. Yet this poem beautifully depicts a scene from this region; it conveys both the silently accumulating whiteness and the sense of calm that comes with it. I remember reading this poem as a boy—in fact, it may have quietly engraved "snow" in my imagination.

Even in the city, we can feel the presence of the falling snow. We can sense it collecting as we sleep tucked into our futons. "Ah, it feels like snow tonight," we say. It is unclear which sense organ perceives this. Perhaps our hearing picks up the way snow muffles sound. The following morning, we look out of the window and see a world transformed, covered in white. Each time I witness this scene I wonder how such a magical phenomenon can occur in the natural world. I feel a desire to have it stay this way for a while longer. Yet, inevitably, footprints and car tracks mar this elegantly white, drifted world. Once this happens, the snow becomes no more than a nuisance.

One last thing about the memory of snow imprinted on me as a boy. It concerns the poem "The Morning of the Last Farewell" by Miyazawa Kenji. On her deathbed, a sister asks her brother, the poet, to get her a handful of "slush." She asks, "Get me some *ameyuju,* will you?" His heart feels about to burst open. The strange request sends him rushing out the door and into the falling sleet "like a stray bullet."

Miyazawa's readers feel both his gratitude and his earnest appeal. He is grateful to be able to respond to his sister's final, humble request. As Miyazawa writes: "From the branches of this glistening pine tree / full of transparent, cold droplets / and holding carefully this pure-white mixture of snow and water / I shall gather / my young sister's final meal." What a painful clarity there is in the words, "Her final meal."

Snow blankets the world in white as if by sacred magic. Were snow any other color, it would certainly have been perceived as something ominous. Yet, through the workings of nature, snow is white. And since white is a color that makes us feel we have brushed up against death, it is only natural that the spectacle of a world covered in snow inspires us with a certain religious emotion. If you magnify snow you discover elaborate crystals. Even more surprising is the infinite variety of shapes these crystals take depending on conditions like temperature and weather in the upper atmosphere. This is why no two snowflakes are alike. Each flake flutters down from the sky in all its absolute uniqueness, one of a multitude falling thick but quiet before settling on the earth.

005 Plaster

There is a certain dampness in the word plaster—in Japanese, 漆喰.
First, I sense a faint moisture in the sound of the word itself—*shikkui*.
There is a theory that the word shikkui was used only to phonetically
replicate the T'ang Chinese pronunciation of the word "lime." Indeed,
the literal meaning of these characters "to eat lacquer"—漆を喰う—is
rather unsettling. In both the West and the East, living environments
were completed by plastering the walls. Plaster has held a significant
role in Japan since ancient times. It was made by mixing and kneading
together powdered limestone and *funori* seaweed or hemp fibers.

It is said that plaster breathes. When the air is humid, plaster
absorbs moisture. And when the air is dry, it releases its water content,
maintaining a constant level of humidity within a room. Thus, the
way plaster breathes provides comfort to us physiologically and even
emotionally: its responsiveness to the environment and the cool moist-
ness of its matte finish seem to offer us a deep sense of calm.

A plasterer is one of the many workers who contribute to the
building of a house. Compared to a carpenter who climbs roofs and
works three-dimensionally, a plasterer's work is flat, without depth,
but impressive all the same. Is it due to the elegant way he handles the
trowel? Or is it because the application of plaster signals that the
house is almost finished?

The funori, or glue plant, is not mixed with the lime powder to
act as an adhesive. Rather, it is to ensure that the mixture attains a
certain viscosity; it makes the plaster soft so that the trowel can apply
it elegantly and smoothly to the wall—a satisfyingly flat surface of
plaster completely spread out over a wall without a single gap. To acquire a technique is to become highly competent in all aspects of a
particular form of work. Thus, techniques of plastering can produce
different results: one may well have a polished gloss, for example,

while another retains subtle traces of the trowel. Yet I believe what makes plaster so special is the satisfying, rolling tactility of its matte finish combined with its high level of visible surface precision. It is best to apply many layers, because it takes as long as half a year for a single coat of plaster to dry completely. And since walls that have had two or three layers applied are stronger and less likely to crack, attaining this ideal for even a single wall can take an extremely large amount of time and labor.

In English, there are many words to describe the color of plaster. It is not merely white. Off-white, lime white, antique white, bone white, new white…. There are even those shades, like "James White," that are named after people. When finishing the walls of a house, do plasterers discuss these subtle nuances of color? Are such names created to show respect for the acquired patina things from past eras, or to distinguish what is seen as antiquated from the new, fresh face of change? In any case, it appears that the different names for the colors of plaster are imbued with a subtle feeling for those parts of the historical past that humanity has deemed important to preserve.

006   Walls

Once, during a period when I did nothing but practice sketching, I read a book called *The Theory of Sketching* by Iwata Yatomi, which included instructions on how to draw walls. Although walls might appear to be ordinary surfaces, Iwata wrote, the light that falls on them is never uniform. Rather, the light reflecting off an object in the room and illuminating the subtly uneven surface of the wall itself produces a vast diversity of shadows. I was sitting in my high school in Okayama preparing for my exams when I read this. I was in the arts studio, in fact, facing several alabaster busts. When I finished reading it, I found myself looking up at the walls of the studio with a fresh perspective.

These busts were lined up in a row in this studio linked to the arts classroom. The background was a plastered wall. And across this wall was a gradation of light—bright near the window and darkening as it extended further into the room. The window was large and sunny, and placed at a right angle to the wall I was observing. As if caressing the wall, the soft light fell obliquely along its surface, exposing minute bumps, impressions, and even blemishes. A wall is never completely flat. Traces of the trowel remain. Even its construction is filled with subtle imperfections. If you direct your awareness towards the physicality of the wall, you recognize lurking shadows and a depth worth drawing—things you would not normally notice when viewing the wall as mere background for the busts. Iwata encourages his readers to closely observe this complexity as a means of practicing sketching.

To see is to observe not only shape but light. And further, to respond to it. Drawing is that response made concrete. Indeed, if you can really foreground a wall by means of the light falling on it, registering all its tiny scars and depressions and other marks, then the majority of your drawing is already finished. That, as far as I remember, was the crux of Iwata's argument teaching.

I do not recall how well I drew that particular studio wall. Yet from then on, I came to see walls as an entity that attracts and houses a spirit—a *yorishiro*—but in this case one that attracts not a spirit, but light. Walls are like photosensitive plates or photographic printing paper that register with precision the light that shines on them.

A dim shaft of light entering through a small window and falling on the wall of a hotel that was once a prison in Amsterdam: this is the kind of light that Johannes Vermeer liked to paint.

The bold shadow of a rhinoceros beetle defined by the naked rays of the sun clings to the wall of an oasis. The light of the Sahara Desert is ferocious, burning away the protective blanket of air.

The light reflecting off the surface of Lake Titicaca flickers across the walls of a lakeside hotel. At close to four thousand meters above sea level, the light is clear in the thin, pellucid atmosphere.

Nor is it just the angle of the sun's rays. Light also changes depending on the levels of dryness or moisture in the atmosphere of a given area of land. The light of the city and that of the seashore are completely different even within the same region.

It seems to me that my memories of light are necessarily coupled with my recollections of that same light reflected off walls.

007 The Houses of Mykonos

Mykonos is a Greek island rising out of the Aegean Sea. Almost all the island's houses have dazzling white walls that glow in the clear, bright sunlight. What explains that vivid white? The light of the Mediterranean plays its part, but it's more than that. Rather, it is because the houses are whitewashed every year, before the arrival of summer.

Walls, no matter how often repainted, will dirty over time. Plaster especially attracts dirt. Keeping the walls spotless for even a single year is difficult. They are touched by hands, exposed to the wind and rain, covered by a thin layer of dust, and pelted by ultraviolet rays. The surface almost imperceptibly shifts to shades of grey and beige. Actually, there is a certain beauty in this transition, one that appeals to Japanese sensibilities, to the quiet appreciation of slow natural alterations—that is, *wabi*—as well as the sort of elegant simplicity that Japanese tend to admire. However, the people of Mykonos spare no effort in meticulously restoring the pure radiance of the walls every year.

It is as if the island were covered in calcium crystals or a bloom of pigmentless mushrooms. Perhaps this cycle of painting and fading is performed as an act in concert with the rhythm of generation and decay intrinsic to the universe—here, a paean to the return of summer. Or perhaps it is simply a manifestation of the will to live.

Apparently, the custom began when a paste of crushed white limestone was painted on the walls to exterminate an infectious disease that plagued the island. The whitewashed houses became a permanent feature of the island, and the color of the architecture was enacted into law in 1975. The result is a coating that has been painstakingly built up over many years. In other words, the walls of the houses of Mykonos are the color of a laminate produced by multiple layers of limestone. What were once sharp edges are now softened;

corners that once intersected at right angles have taken on sleepy, rounded curves. The accumulation of this calcareous membrane has slowly transformed the houses and churches, so that they seem covered in a pale sugary glaze—chalk-white Baumkuchen cakes basking in the sunlight of the Aegean Sea.

This year, before summer comes, they will apply yet another layer of plaster. It is an infinite overlap of opaque membranes—white on white on white; layers upon layers of matte white.

The blueness of the backdrop of the sky and the ocean also throws the houses of Mykonos into relief. The blue of the Aegean Sea does not leave a misty impression like the blues of Japan. It is the unmistakable ultramarine of a calm ocean, of a clear and brilliant sky. Such a blue does not require metaphors or abstractions like "it is a blue bluer than the bluest blue." It simply manifests before you, unfurling right before your eyes. The island's white architecture stands out sharply against this background.

When I was twenty years old I wandered the world for about two months. I stopped by Mykonos on a whim along the way. A single jump from Athens on a propeller plane. The airport was the definition of simplicity; it looked shabby, almost like a roofed bus shelter. Very few people got off. Those of us who did climbed into the open cargo bed of an old four-wheel drive military truck and were carried off to town. As we left the high lying airport and descended towards the coast, the town that lay before us took my breath away.

008   The Evergreen Magnolia

I have the photographer Ishimoto Yasuhiro's *Evergreen Magnolia* hanging on the wall of my study. The fleshy, plump petals of the flowers somehow remind me of edible lily bulbs—they seem filled with the weightiness of life. Every time I look at the photograph I feel myself grow calm. Ishimoto's "Katsura Imperial Villa" series is extremely famous. Sadly, just when I thought I would like to go and visit Ishimoto, he passed away. The Katsura Villa is indeed a beautiful work of architecture. Yet, after visiting the Villa several times, I have come to believe that its true beauty is seen in the way it is expressed through photography rather than in the actual buildings themselves.

Ishimoto was born in San Francisco but moved to his parents' hometown in Japan when he was three years old. He then lived in Kōchi Prefecture until he graduated from high school. Not long after that he returned to America. During the Second World War, he was forced to live in a Japanese-American internment camp in Colorado. It was there that he came across photography. He was exposed to pioneering studies of visual art like László Moholy-Nagy's *Vision in Motion* and György Kepes's *Language of Vision*. Moholy-Nagy, after escaping the Nazis, had helped found the New Bauhaus school of art and design, seeking to create a new world. He taught at the school but passed away suddenly soon after it opened. The school was assimilated into the Illinois Institute of Technology after his death. In fact, this institute was established in Chicago by the last president of Bauhaus, Ludwig Mies van der Rohe. After the war, Ishimoto Yasuhiro studied at Chicago's New Bauhaus school. I am not sure if Ishimoto was aware of this, but the education he received on American soil was a direct legacy from the original Bauhaus—an unexpected baptism into modernism.

When Ishimoto returned to Japan, he was commissioned to take photographs of the Katsura Imperial Villa. Chance connections continued to lead him along fortunate paths. The photobook *Katsura* was co-supervised by Walter Gropius and Tange Kenzō, who were among the founders of Bauhaus. And the book itself was designed by Herbert Bayer, a lecturer at Bauhaus. It was around this time that the three-hundred-year-old Katsura Villa was being showered with praise by pioneering modernists such as Bruno Taut and Gropius. However, Tange, a leader of the Japanese architectural community at the time, appears to have been somewhat discomfited by this praise. To appreciate the merits of traditional Japanese architecture, he believed, one has to reach a true understanding of it, including its origins, its flesh and bones, so to speak. He considered Katsura Villa the crowning achievement of *Japanese* architecture, whether seen from a modernist or traditional perspective. On the other hand, tradition is often scorned by those whose sights are set on the future.

Ishimoto was a photographer who combined Japanese sensibility with a modernist intelligence. I expect he understood Tange's reservations. I imagine Katsura Villa, as evoked in this splendid collection of photographs, will continue to act as the background for many more equally fruitful interactions and encounters.

The petals of Ishimoto's "Evergreen Magnolia" are calm and quiet—the graceful whiteness of a Japanese flower chosen by the photographer who memorialized Katsura. You can almost smell its sweet fragrance.

009 Sheep

The movements of a flock of sheep. I sometimes witness this in my travels. Though they bring traffic to a standstill, I remain composed, for I sense in each passing sheep an eagerness to keep up with the herd characteristic of timid animals. "Ah," I think to myself, "let's just let them pass." There is something touching about the dynamic produced by a flock of pack animals—a chain of all weak links, so to speak. And yet, despite being clad in white, the sheep are always so terribly dirty. The feeling of clarity I expect from whiteness is absent.

I once caught sight of a flock of sheep from a low-flying airplane. They were only a small part of an expansive vista, a truly peaceful, pastoral scene, you would think. Yet the sight made me feel vaguely uncomfortable. The sheep looked like rice grains spilling across a grass-covered plain. Other animals—alpacas in the Andes, for example—blend into their surroundings naturally, even though they are clearly out grazing on a pasture. So why, then, did I have such a strange reaction to the sheep?

You can have clean towels, but not clean sheep. White is so easily soiled that it is not surprising that sheep are always dirty. But long ago, they were tawny, black, or even deep brown, like alpacas and camels. It was humans who deprived them of their color.

The relationship between sheep and humans is long. It is estimated that sheep were being raised as far back as 7,000 to 6,000 BCE in Mesopotamia. Every part of the sheep served a purpose in the lives of those peoples. Meat, wool, milk, even skin. The hide could be made into parchment.

Wild sheep used to grow two layers of wool, thick and coarse on top, fine and soft underneath. However, it appears repeated breeding led to a sheep that possessed only the soft, easy-to-use inner fleece. Eventually, white, which can be dyed any color, selectively remained. This occurred alongside the evolution of dyeing techniques. Molded by the demands of humanity, domesticated sheep were now far from wild; their nature had changed.

Early fourteenth-century Spain was where today's merino sheep were bred. Thanks to their success breeding a sheep with nothing but an extremely delicate and long fleece, Spain held the leading position in wool exports for some time. Eventually, merino sheep spread across the world. Today's key wool industries in Australia and New Zealand were launched at the end of the eighteenth century based on the new merino breed.

Thus, the view of innumerable white sheep moving over natural hills and fields is actually quite distant from "nature." Perhaps if they exhibited their original colors, the scene would strike us as soothing since those colors would still be connected to the surrounding environment. Instead we witness animals clad in the history of their exploitation, bred for their meat, wool, milk, and hide. And so, the obedient flocks appear somehow melancholic, stained by the selfishness of human beings.

There comes a time for sheep to be sheared. The shearing is executed beautifully by skilled workers, though the sheep, of course, are anything but happy about it. They bleat pitifully as if to ask that their wool not be taken from them. But it is no use. Their fate is sealed. The moment the shears cut through the fleece, a snowy whiteness emerges from underneath the dirtied wool. After the shearing is finished, the sheep look so thin and forlorn that you could mistake them for some other animal, their peach-colored skin visible in gaps where the fleece was sheared away completely.

010   Salt Flats

The Uyuni Salt Flat of Bolivia is a magnificent plain of salt about two-thirds the area of Shikoku, the smallest of the four main Japanese islands—about the size of Lake Ontario in Canada. Over an enormously long time, sea salt was lifted by the movements of the Andes mountain range and deposited at a height of 3,700 meters above sea level. The flats look "perfectly level"—an expression that is always misleading—and in fact the elevation across this area varies by only a few dozen centimeters. Thus, we can believe our eyes and call this area perfectly level. If we turn about, we are surrounded by a salt flat that stretches to the horizon on all sides.

During the day the rays of the sun are strong and hot; at night it is cold. Although the flat resembles a desert, the difference lies in the fact there are places covered with water. In the dry areas, the endless flat surface is covered by striated protrusions that resemble the rough stripes in the skin of a melon, forming a repeated hexagonal pattern just large enough to fit both feet into. Perhaps this is due to the way salt crystallizes.

The areas covered with water maintain a consistent depth of about ten centimeters. You can walk anywhere with a pair of boots. The salty water does not turn to ice even at below-freezing temperatures. Perhaps because the thick brine is relatively dense, the water's surface is still, without even the tiniest ripple. This unmoving surface becomes a mirror—the clouds above it are reflected in perfect symmetry. On the evening of a full moon, when both sun and moon are floating in the sky at opposite ends of the horizon, both are reflected in the water. Thus, you witness four heavenly bodies suspended within a single field of vision. It is easy to be drawn into the illusion that you are no longer on earth but some totally different planet. The illusion is so convincing that it seems strange to even be able to breathe.

It was a photo shoot that brought me to this place. The location team was a unit of three four-wheel-drive vehicles, so I was not completely alone. Yet when I walked straight ahead for ten minutes, the others looked as small as poppy seeds, so small that it became impossible to know what they were doing. Answering the call of nature thus became a simple matter—you just become a poppy seed and do it. The sense of isolation on such occasions was particularly striking.

From the music I had brought with me, I chose to listen to "Ave Maria" sung by the countertenor Slava Vyatcheslav Kagan-Paley. I wanted to see what it was like to walk over a sea of clouds with his solo filling my ears. The heavenly voice of the artist and the exquisite surrounding scenery fused into one. Only the clouds moved. The rest stood still. I suddenly thought: perhaps the next world is a far lonelier place than I expected.

In certain conditions of light, this mirror on the surface of the earth transforms into the seven prismatic colors. Sunrise and sunset are especially dramatic. We decided to photograph the area at dawn, and so, relying on our GPS, we tracked down the spot we planned to shoot from and waited in the darkness. Before long the world began to dimly glow. From the horizon line emerged in parallel deep blue, green, red, light purple, and again a deep blue—an *obi* of light rising above and falling below the horizon in line after line of thin gradations of color. Soon the horizon formed a boundary, a line from which a sea of clouds emerged, and our entire world, both sky and ground, was dyed rose red. White is not the absence of color. Rather, it is fully saturated with it. I came to understand this the moment I stood stock still within an overflowing flood of color.

011 Shōji

The faint background presence of *shōji* always comes to mind whenever I think of Japanese interior spaces. Shōji filters naked light into a soft glow unlike any other screen or shade. The illumination is diffused and made uniform by the fibers in the rough Japanese paper. Thus, light is invited into the room by the glowing "surface" that is shōji. In Japanese buildings, which have long, outstretched eaves, direct sunlight does not reach indoors. What enters the home is the indirect light reflecting off the garden and surrounding environment. Shōji filters this weakened light even further, bringing it indoors as a modest glow diffused by the texture of the Japanese paper.

Compared to glass, paper is thin and light. Shōji paper is affixed to the slender lattice frame with glue. Once attached, it is moistened with a spray. The paper first expands, then shrinks as it dries, achieving a secure, uniform tension. This "tautness," as though charged with life, extends across the entire lattice frame creating a pleasant tension. It is incredible to think that such a durable structure is held together by nothing but a thin paper membrane. A shōji is light enough to be lifted in one hand. And yet its elegance, taut from end to end, heightens our awareness of our surroundings.

While the long fibers of shōji paper are strong in themselves, they aren't able to resist damage by extreme forces. A sharp poke with your index finger will put a hole in the shōji. One comes to see the subtlety of Japanese life when considering what it takes to construct a house with such fragile furnishings. The shōji defines inner space by maintaining a taut surface that is at once thin and fragile, light yet even, distributing this tension to every corner of its frame. There is a stubborn paradox in this—a weakness that, stretched to the limit, forms a strength.

A rowdy or rough demeanor cannot be tolerated within this atmosphere. Perhaps the shōji and sliding interior *fusuma* stimulate something within us. The fragile yet precise enclosures of space that they create threatens to collapse at the slightest outbreak of rude behavior. Perhaps Japanese physicality has been disciplined by this particular form of room partitioning, our manners inculcated through its influence.

On the grounds of Jishō-ji—also known as Ginkaku-ji or the Temple of the Silver Pavilion—there is a hall called the Tōgu-dō. Within the Tōgu-dō sits a *shoin*—a study—called Dōjinsai. Jishō-ji, built by Ashikaga Yoshimasa as his villa in the middle of the Muromachi Period played a central role in Kyoto's Higashiyama culture. Yoshimasa spent much of his time in this four-and-a-half-tatami-sized study. A desk for writing and reading directly faces a shōji-adorned window. Shōji also make up the wall to the right. The walls behind and to the left of the desk are fusuma. And directly on the left-hand side of the desk is a set of staggered shelves. The study is simplicity itself. Yet, as soon as you sit at the desk, your back straightens, and your senses become hyper-acute as if straining to receive the slightest of impressions. Quietly, the light entering through these various screens registers deep in your senses. It is as if some faint blessing is soaking into your skin.

"I see," I say to myself. So, this is how we Japanese came to develop the concept of *ma* / 間—that is, space or interval. My instincts have guided me to this and other realizations about Japanese-style spaces.

012　Boxes

Boxes are magical things. Even the most ordinary object is made splendid when placed in a box. Highly valuable lacquerware, ceramics, or porcelain—for example, vessels prized in the tea ceremony—are arranged in a box of plain unvarnished wood that suits their aesthetic. Inscriptions, giving the origin of the piece or other identifying information, are written in calligrapher's ink on the top and underside of the box's lid. A lining is carefully applied, and the ware is covered with a fabric corresponding to its shape. Sometimes even an insect-repellent turmeric-infused cloth is draped over the object—this being the definition of lavish ostentatiousness. Once the lid is closed, even shaking the box will produce not even the slightest rattle. A box that rattles, however, cannot be relied on to fulfill its protective function. Even a mismatched collection is elevated when splendidly displayed in a well-designed and perfectly sized box.

A woven striped braid is used to tie up the paulownia-wood box. Different striped patterns can be requested when ordering the braid. The skill it took to make the distinctive braid and the design that gives each cord its depth are hidden from view within each strand.

The paulownia tree is resistant to both fire and water. Apparently, antique vessels have been so well preserved in Japan thanks to the custom of using paulownia boxes. On the other hand, boxes made of unfinished wood—in Japanese, "white wood" 白木—are themselves delicate. The effects of wear and tear show up conspicuously on their soft, pure surface: their corners chip easily, and they become black and soiled from age and long handling. This danger always lurks just beneath such a box's surface. There are boxes so worn that their inscriptions are almost indecipherable. Yet, the moment they are tied with wonderfully stylish strings we once again fall under their spell. Indeed, any ware that emerges from such a box will possess a dignified aura.

There is a phrase *mottai o tsukeru*—meaning "to lend an air of importance to"—that describes how boxes can confer a sense of grace or dignity on their contents. Boxes have been tools devised over time specifically to convey such an "air." *Ido* and *raku* ware, types of inscribed tea ceremony cups, are a good example of this. Ido cups were introduced to Japan via Korea, where they were made for everyday use. They are a light orange, the color of loquat, and simple. They carry within that simplicity a bottomless well of sentiment favored by masters of the tea ceremony, and thus were seen to possess a high value. Raku tea cups were made by Sasaki Chōjirō, a master tile-maker, at the request of Sen no Rikyū. A raku cup fits so snugly in your hand that it is easy to forget it is there. These cups also stand at the pinnacle of simplicity. Both ido and raku ware were prized for their elegant simplicity and the beauty of their refined irregularity. The aesthetic principles that established this tradition have been transmitted from generation to generation, and the dense patterns and subtle techniques embodied in these vessels speak eloquently of their intrinsic value—hence they are now seen as having an "air of importance." Yet when ido, raku or other prized wares are left out of their boxes, the uninitiated may treat them as everyday clutter, occasionally even going so far as to throw them away. Thus the boxes, with their own "air of importance," have silently borne the responsibility of protecting the cups' value.

Such is the power of boxes. It is also why boxes can deceive people. A valueless item in an impressive box may entice the unwary. The Japanese fascination with boxes, a continuing love that stretches beyond antique art, is perhaps tied to such a history, to the way that *mottai o tsukeru* has been cultivated.

013   Hakuji

There is a general word in Japanese for ceramics: literally "ceramic-and-porcelainware." However, ceramic and porcelain are in fact quite different. While traces of the earth remain in ceramic, porcelain seems to have transcended its earthly origins. As if, by surviving a temperature that surpassed some critical point, it has regenerated as a completely new substance: earth transmuted into a semi-transparent form.

In China, where porcelain was first made, this sweetly green-white, semi-transparent stone-like material came to be prized as a jewel. In fact, it has been called "a precious stone" since ancient times. Porcelain beckons light inward. Its vague mystery has been used in a variety of settings—from the personal accessories of the nobility to the instruments of ritual. It has been theorized that porcelain was first fired with the intent to create a "jewel bowl," an assumption that may not be misplaced.

The idea of baking earth to produce a jewel resembles alchemy. The great pains taken by alchemists in their attempts to produce gold from other materials may seem like a waste of effort on first glance. Yet even if no alchemist ever succeeded in creating gold, the unending quest to do so resulted in discoveries of even greater value. It is said that the true gold is the process itself. Distilled liquor, many kinds of medicine, perhaps even the discipline of chemistry are all fruits of the alchemists' endless trial and error.

In similar fashion, what was created was not the jewel that was sought after, but porcelain. Porcelain is fired at relatively high temperatures, possesses no water absorbency, and emits a metallic clink when struck with a fingernail. The celadon porcelain of China's Song dynasty, a particularly splendid example, emanates serenity and grace. Compared with the porcelainware of the following dynasties, with their gaudy decorations, celadon ware is dignified and intellectual. The word "refinement" seems particularly apt in its case. This is especially true of the *ru* variety of celadon of the late Northern Song dynasty, renowned for having "the color of the sky just after the rain." One feels that the charm of ru ware, with its subdued, almost literary melancholy, surpasses even that of a jewel bowl.

In *hakuji* or "white porcelain," which appeared around the same time as celadon ware, the glaze sometimes has a glass-like finish, and sometimes the clay itself has been fired into a semi-transparent glass. Hakuji originates from what is called "Blue Flower" pottery—which is white, decorated with indigo-blue patterns. It was the most popular form of pottery throughout the Ming dynasty. It then became the foundation of hakuji, whose whiteness may have been intensified to highlight the indigo. One particularly celebrated area, Jingdezhen in China, produced outstanding hakuji using porcelain stone from the nearby Kaolin mountain. It was around that time that kilns supplying ware to be presented to the emperor were first designated "official kilns." As an export item, too, hakuji was exceedingly successful. The Blue Flower pottery that influenced Nabeshima and early Imari in Japan used the same bright white as its background. In the Qing dynasty, the decorative painting became still more colorful, further intensifying the rich colors of the porcelain.

I have visited the illustrious Jingdezhen potteries several times in recent years and have realized time and again that hakuji without any painted decorations are the most beautiful. The unadorned skin of the jewel, so to speak. To someone like me, who has always preferred quiet refinement, that is, *wabi*, the most desirable porcelain objects are those that lack drawings. Only the best hakuji turn beautifully transparent when held up to the light. I find myself enraptured. Put tea in it and its color becomes all the brighter. Whenever I meet a Zen priest friend of mine, he always gives me a refined hakuji cup with a subdued gloss. I use these cups exclusively to drink sake. Sake drunk from them is truly refreshing.

014   Joseon Dynasty Ceramics

We must not forget Korean ceramics. When I come face to face with the white of Joseon dynasty porcelain, I feel a sudden release of tension as the stress of everyday life leaves my heart. I gaze with fascination at its texture—I feel the urge to touch it. I long to pick it up, put it down by my side, use it. Applying the word "personality" to ceramics may seem strange, but Joseon porcelain gives me the kind of relief and comfort that I associate with the presence of a good friend who accepts me just as I am. This feeling must be due to the porcelain's smooth surface, so receptive to the comings and goings of things, and to the drowsy quality of its white color.

In the fifteenth century, during the transition from the Goryeo to the Joseon dynasty, porcelain with a distinctive whiteness appeared. Gray, unglazed pottery was dipped in a watery white clay mixture called an engobe over which a transparent glaze was drizzled. Then, the vessels were re-fired. Based on the differing techniques used to apply this engobe, the results are variously called "Three Island," "flour-dusted," or "brush-marked" pottery in Japan. *Hakuji*, on the other hand, with its transparent white glaze applied to white, unglazed pottery, matured during the long-lasting Joseon dynasty. It is said that the strongly Confucian culture of the period prized the color white for its perceived purity. And indeed, we see the jade-colored celadon ware, characteristic of Goryeo extravagance, gradually relax into a tasteful white during the Joseon, until it finally becomes a white of astounding depth. The snow whites influenced by Ming Blue Flower ware, the grays of what is called *katade* ware, the milk whites with their plump glazes, and whites tinged with a slight blue-green that give the porcelain a cold dignity—each and every one of these whites has its own depths, its own distinctive character.

The charm of ceramics and porcelain lies in the space between artifice and nature. No matter how perfectly an individual artist does his or her work, defects and irregularities in the clay expand and become visible after they are exposed to fire. These characteristics materialize as unpredictable distortions and variations of color. Being a potter, I expect, means learning to accept whatever imperfections may come.

However, such deviations were strictly prohibited in China's official kilns. Perhaps because they were made to reflect the power of the imperial authority, one senses in these wares a tenacious dedication that attempts to gain complete mastery of all the subtleties of pottery: an attempt, in other words, to have clay submit to the human intellect and will—much as a large corporation disallows even the slightest flaw in its products. Perhaps this is not unlike the way a company boss looks to save face by laying the blame for an inadvertent error on a worker, instead of apologizing himself. By contrast, Joseon kilns resembled smaller companies, recognizing that it was the fate of ceramics to be at the mercy of nature, and accepting tremors of the hand and the fluctuations of fire. This was also reflected in the pottery used by the common people in their daily life. Further away, on the other side of the sea, in Japan, these natural flaws were well received and even valued. To Japanese of the late Muromachi era, on the brink of discovering the beauty in refined simplicity (*wabi*) and impermanence (*susabi*), such accident and distortion shimmered with potential.

Yet white pottery was not admired in Japan at that time. Rather, the loquat-colored tea bowls of the *ido* or "water-well" style claimed all the attention. Not until some time later was the beauty of white recognized in everyday pottery. It has even been argued that it was through Joseon ceramics that the great art historian Yanagi Muneyoshi (1889–1961) came to understand *mingei*, the name he coined for Japanese folk art.

In pottery, the accidental may enhance beauty, but if overemphasized may also create a miserable, ugly shape. Joseon porcelain's charm lies in how it balances between attention to detail and the refusal of perfection.

015   Soy Sauce Cruets

And amongst porcelain, we also must not forget the food bowls, the dishes and the tiny pitchers called "cruets" used for soy sauce—those daily necessities mass-produced as industrial goods. The word "ceramics" tends to suggest a single, handcrafted item, something with a well-established artistic value. Yet quantity and stability make up the beauty of everyday life. Of course, Japanese cultural aesthetics exalts distortion and the mark of the hand, but mass-produced ceramics are what support our small daily joys.

Product designer Mori Masahiro was a man who dedicated all his energy to the production of *hakuji* (white porcelain ware) as an industrial good in Hasami, Nagasaki. He served forty years as a member of the Japan Design Committee, whose members are architects, designers, and critics. As a young man, though, before he became a member, he apparently submitted his soy sauce cruet design countless times to the Matsuya Ginza design collection. He did this until it was finally selected by the Committee. With each rejection, he asked which part of his design was lacking. He modified this precise aspect and promptly re-entered the design. Today, the cruet design that was finally selected has become the standard in Japan. Yet, more than just a design standard, it is familiar to all as a staple of daily use. It is a masterpiece, known the way a famous piece of poetry is known—everyone recognizes it without ever knowing its author.

I once visited Mori's workshop in Hasami. During our conversation he remarked: "When people are told that right here in the heart of the area famous for its ceramics, tens of thousands of mass-produced items are also manufactured, they tend to trivialize them, right? It's the one-of-a-kind, hand-made 'works of art' going for hundreds of dollars that are most admired. If you make mass-produced, cheaply priced items, they just won't get the same respect. But, listen, you can't really be called an industry unless you produce goods that can be continually sold by the thousands."

Mori chose Hasami as his home base because it is rich in a crucial raw material called Amakusa stone. Now it is the center of hakuji production in Japan. Even now, I hear the things he told me echoing in my ears. "Stay at a luxury ryokan in Kyoto and they'll serve you fine rice in very light, small, thin bowls. The way I feel, though, a rice bowl for everyday use should be a little thicker and simpler. Such things give us a greater sense of stability. Rice served up in those kinds of bowls looks that much more delicious."

Design is sincerity manifested in infinite iterations—that's what I learned from Mori's approach to making things. The beauty of ceramics is not limited to the masterpieces of tea pottery. It is in the small teapots and teacups, the rice bowls and soy sauce cruets. It is in the quality of mass-produced products that the true beauty of a country's design is to be found.

As I walked around Mori's workshop, my eye fell on a sake serving flask that resembled an enlarged soy sauce cruet. *Wow, that's great*, I thought, staring in admiration. Mori then suddenly said, "Why don't you take that one home with you?" and kindly made me a gift of it on the spot. Whenever I bring out this hakuji flask, just like that, I find myself sipping sake and remembering Mori Masahiro.

016   Rice Bowls

Rice is the staple food of the Japanese. Cooked rice is placed in a bowl. We then raise that bowl to our mouths and eat. The culture of taking up bowls in the hand may be limited to Japan. Since our historical custom was to eat at low tables while sitting on tatami, I suppose it was only natural that we also came to lift up our dishes—rice bowls, soup bowls, small kobachi bowls and the like. Even when we left the tatami to take on "the daily life of the chair," we Japanese never took our hands from our bowls. We have retained this rare custom even now, after surveying the world and its manners. Using the hand opposite the one holding chopsticks, we support the bowl securely between forefinger and pinky. The thumb naturally supports the edge of the bowl. Eating with a straight back while taking care not to bring one's mouth close to the food—this is part of what it means to conduct oneself in a humble, reserved manner.

The fact that each person possesses his or her own unique bowl is also interesting. In my own household, my wife, my son and I each have one rice bowl we use exclusively. We do not use bowls from the same set. The color, patterns, size, even the type of ceramic are different.

I was in my mid-thirties when I first came to choose my own bowl, a *yokinoyaki* from Tanegashima. While traveling, I fell in love with this elegant high-fired and unglazed bowl that resembled those from Bizen. Thinking I would like to make it a kind of life companion, I brought it home with me. It was a most elegant bowl. I hoped it would help me appear dignified. I suppose I thought it would help me acquire a certain fatherly presence. As I gradually gained weight, though, I came to wonder if the bowl was not a little too big. Of course, simply adding less rice to the bowl would have solved the problem, but this proved to be not so simple in practice.

Looking for a bowl of more humble size, I obtained a half-spherical Arita bowl covered in a *tako-kurakusa* ("octopus arabesque") pattern.

I came across this piece in an antique porcelain shop on Furumonzen Road in Kyoto. It quickly became my favorite, and when my wife accidentally broke it, I ordered a replacement from the same store, an even smaller bowl than the first one. I had by this time come to admire the indigo of blue-and-white porcelain, something I had not done as a young man, and to appreciate the dense *tako-kurakusa* style. This bowl is part of the historical development of *hakuji* ware, so its interior is without adornment. Rice fits nicely in the white space of the bowl held up by my left hand. This was when I was in my forties.

Life moved along in this way until I came across an angular hakuji bowl in a city called Takeo in Saga Prefecture. It was essentially a half-sphere, with sides cut away to form an octagon. My left hand, so used to the smooth, rounded base of porcelain, was pleased by the audacious shape. Such encounters always occur during my travels—there is never time to think things over. I boldly bought two, one large and one small. And my rice bowls become smaller still.

Even now I use these two the most. My son has long since moved out of the family home and so, with my wife, there is no longer any need for "fatherly dignity." Moreover, now that I am past fifty, I have to limit my carbohydrates even further. When I am asked, "Which bowl is it today?" I would like to say, "The big one," knowing that this "big" bowl is already relatively small. And yet, resisting further, I say, "I'll take the small one." But what I am really thinking, as I take up my small rice bowl? *Ah, I'm going to get myself a mountain of rice in a huge bowl. It's high time I gave myself permission to stuff my face!*

017   Eggs

I once thought that all eggs were white, but I have had to correct this impression. Perhaps because I have the habit of eating chicken's eggs almost every day, or perhaps because the impressive, rough, ivory-white of ostrich eggs had been burned into my mind, I equated all eggs with white. And believing that, I would look at variously colored and patterned eggs and see only white. Unknowingly, I had internalized a false perception: that in general, eggs are simply white, like bones, milk and such. And so, I saw white eggs.

But if you stop and look more objectively, you will soon realize that the eggs you are eating come in a variety of colors. It seems that eggs by and large come from a white-feathered chicken called the White Leghorn. Recently, however, one sees reddish-brown eggs more often. Since these eggs are always sold at a slightly higher price, with names that appear to carry some special significance, I had assumed that they were from some chickens given a special kind of feed. But, like the Cochin chickens of Nagoya, it seems, chickens with reddish-brown plumage simply lay eggs whose colors match their feathers. Apparently, the difference in the price of these eggs is due to the quality and amount of feed the chickens receive, as well as the rarity of the breed. In other words, the difference has almost nothing to do with the eggs themselves.

The Araucana chicken lays light-green or light-blue eggs. The eggs of the emu are a deep green, sometimes so dark they appear black. Crows' eggs are not black like their feathers but have brownish speckles on a pale blue background.

Conversely, it seems that even if a brown bird lays a brown egg, the concentration of color is influenced by the environment of its parents. "Raise them in a dark, lightless environment," chicken breeders say, "and you get dark brown; raise them in the bright outdoors, you get light-brown." Of course, quail and many other birds' eggs exhibit camouflage patterns—colors that help them escape the eyes of their natural predators by mimicking the living environments of the birds. The shape of an egg makes laying it easy and rolling it difficult; it is strong against external impacts, weak against internal ones. It made sense when this was explained to me—it follows the logic of color. Does that mean white eggs have given up their defense against predators? Or is their whiteness a result of human intervention?

When I was in high school, my biology teacher asked me: "You! What happens when you apply heat to protein?" Nervously, I replied, "I don't know, I've never heated any protein." "All right, I'll change the question, then," the teacher said with a wry smile. "What happens when you apply heat to an egg?" "Right, well it, um, hardens. No wait, solidifies."

That's right. Boil an egg, peel off its shell and what you find inside is a smooth, pure white substance. This is true across the board, from brown eggs to quail eggs. Perhaps my original impression that all eggs were white came from the appearance of boiled and peeled eggs. I had thought that "chicken's child white," a traditional color of Japan, was derived from the shell of chicken's eggs, but this may in fact refer to the color of heated protein.

018   White Peaches

"The peach tree is blooming." So begins a Chinese poem from the *Shijing* or Book of Odes. I think of this poem every time I eat a white peach, because to me it conveys the fruit's essential quality with great accuracy. I am not sure what peaches were like in ancient China when this poem was composed, but when we hear "ripened peaches" in Japan today, we think specifically of white peaches, which even at their ripest have not the slightest tinge of red. Their flesh is a dim green within a faint yellow, and they feel heavy in the hand. I believe this weight relates to the amount of juice they contain. Their sensual flesh is enveloped in a downy, easily blemished skin.

When the fruit is in season, you can peel the skin off with your hand. Covered as it is with fine fuzz, the peach looks as though haloed by light when lifted up. Pinch the bottom—the part with no crease—with the tips of your nails and gently tug. You will find that the skin pulls away ever so thinly and cleanly. The exposed flesh will be plump and slightly wet. Peeling a peach perfectly requires both skill and concentration, since a hard push on the flesh will cause it to bruise and darken. The trick is to work slowly and peel off the largest amount of skin you can each time. But be careful: if you remove too much too hastily you will be left with a peach covered in bruises.

When I do manage to peel away the skin cleanly, without blemish or bruise, I feel very tempted to bite into the peach just as it is, then and there. And of course, that's a fine way to eat it. However, if possible, it's even better to slice the peach carefully and serve it on a plate. Not only is this method more elegant, it is more suitable for relishing this fruit, soft fragrance and all. The problem here is how to cut it. The best way is to insert the knife carefully and cut along the edge of the pit at the heart of the fruit. Further, it is essential to understand how to cut the fruit into as few slices as possible. Slicing up the naturally plump, round peach into tiny angular pieces is a disservice to the fruit. If you set out with a basic plan to divide the flesh into three large slices, things will go well. However, the red area near the pit has very little sweetness—in fact, it tends to be bitter. Therefore, although I have said you should cut along the edge of the pit, your knife must not come into contact with it. Ideally, you will be left with large segments of white peach, having cut away whiteness only, leaving the fruit's curved surface intact.

The plate on which these slices are placed can be glass, *hakuji*, Joseon, or Delft. If possible, the peach should be eaten with a silver dessert fork. Having taken such pains to preserve the integrity of the fruit, you should put down the knife and use a fork to pierce, not cut, each slice. Spear the peach slice in the center on the flat side that was cut off by the knife's blade, gaze at its roundness, then pop it into your mouth.

One reason we should refrain from eating the entire peach whole, without cutting it into segments, is that our hand would become covered in juice, and that juice would be wasted—what a shame that would be! The main reason, however, is that the scent of the peach would be squandered. Piercing it with the fork and putting it into your mouth—it is in this moment that your nose is hit with a truly delightful, calming, sweet fragrance—it lifts me to great heights.

019 Daikon

The poet Naka Tarō wrote, "I will cleanly uproot language, just as I would a daikon from the ground." I think this poem, which I first came across in university, had a long-lasting effect on my perception of both "language" and "daikon."

Language feeds off our experience. It grows, little by little, within our minds. Like seeds sprinkled in the soil of memory, words germinate unnoticed until, suddenly, we find that they have sprouted into a thick tangle of lush green leaves. A daikon in the earth develops even more secretly and quietly, nourished by the earth, just as our language is nourished by experiences that come to us sometimes like rain, sometimes like frost, and most of all like sleep. The daikon grows and fattens. The harvested words are lined up in dictionaries like vegetables in supermarkets. But wild, living words grow in the space-time of our memories without our full awareness. Just like a daikon, a white mass burgeoning in the dark earth....

The poet is aware of the ecology of language and the patterns of verbal development in people's minds. Observing this growth, he skillfully digs up words, like daikon out of the earth, and lines them up before us. We are then surprised and fascinated by these round, plump words that emerged from within our unconscious. We take a timid nibble of this language, delight in its sweetness, and then relish its pungency.

Pulling a white mass like a daikon out of the earth must, I imagine, be truly fulfilling. Calling fat legs "daikon legs" is unkind and derogatory, but the daikon's form, a long, smooth, moderately plump shape, is in fact pleasing, as well as perfectly suited to being extracted from the ground.

Daikon sprout multiple shoots that are sometimes thought to resemble human limbs. Daikon skin has a peculiar tautness; one can feel the growth pushing from the inside out. Perhaps the reason these forked daikon look human is not only due to their shape, but also because we feel a certain affinity with their protrusions. Recently, a daikon that resembled a person running was dubbed "the Escaping Daikon," and became a popular image after photographs of it hanging on a string were taken. I laughed like a child when I saw one picture of it being barked at by a dog. One could easily forget the string was there, and so it looked as if the daikon was fleeing helter-skelter from a harsh, cruel world.

Daikon is eaten boiled, steamed, dried, pickled, and chopped. The best of all, I must say, is grated daikon.

Grate a mountain of daikon and fill a *nabe* pot with it. Adding water and nothing else, turn on the fire, and wait for the pot to boil. Throw in some thinly sliced pork and whatever other ingredients you like. This shabu-shabu-style dish is absolutely delicious. Grating translucent strips from this "bounty of the earth," so white and plump —what a poetic, perfect way to enjoy food. And with that, the daikon does indeed escape, disappearing into the pot.

020 Pearls

The birth of a pearl is shrouded in mystery. Mollusks have an organ called a "mantle," which evolved specifically to produce shell. When a tiny piece of foreign matter finds its way into the inner body of a mollusk, the mantle coats the material in a shiny, glossy substance called nacre, which is identical to that which makes up the shell. The result is a pearl.

My understanding was that pearls are the result of the generative power of the shell itself, which gradually encloses the foreign matter, and I thought that this process in some way harmed the mollusk. If a speck of dirt gets into the human eye, it can simply be washed out, but such a thing is not possible for the handless mollusk. Wrapped in the shell substance, the foreign matter is retained as a part of the body, transformed into something like a hard, round teardrop.

That, at least, was what I presumed. In reality, though, it seems that the main intrusions are fragments that were once part of the mantle itself, and not any piece of foreign matter. The strange and mysterious part is the glow. Its shine is not hard and glittering like a diamond. The iridescent glossiness seems to cast a halo of light around a calm, but very important area of our hearts—like the essence of a smile. Ancient peoples who found pearls—objects created naturally, and only by chance, within the life-world of a mollusk, and therefore very rare at the time—must have been spellbound by this magical feeling.

We have learned since that only certain types of mollusks produce pearls, and that any core material inserted into their tissue will be made into pearl. The result is the cultured pearl. Although not as rare as natural pearls, which are found in only one or two out of ten thousand mollusks, cultured pearls are still "mollusk-made" rather than strictly "man-made." The Japanese pearl industry was built on this distinction.

Of course, there are many kinds of pearls, from the large, bead-like pearls of the South Seas to irregular or "baroque" pearls. They also take on a variety of hues, from snow white to ashen gray. Some are even tinged with red. And just when you thought pearls only had subtle gradations of white, you find there are glistening jet-black pearls also. There are even pearls so very small they look like poppy seeds. Stringing together such tiny pearls to make an ornament requires a very large number of pearls and piercing a hole through each one is such intricate work that it does not seem possible that human beings can do it. And yet, thanks to the dexterity of the human hand, the job is done—exclusively by teenagers with good eyes.

To my mind, the best pearls start and end with glistening white. I think a moderately long necklace of splendidly arranged and painstakingly selected white pearls is truly beautiful. Their restrained luster conveys both quiet decorum and an atmosphere of elegant ceremony. One feels as though the pearls are a sign that some wonderful thing is about to begin.

Research shows that the Japanese of the Middle Ages had a concept, *kizen*, which refers to "the domain of the not-yet-happened," a sense of happiness soon to be born. A pearl's light is kizen: more than just blessing its possessor with radiance or revealing an already present happiness, it seems to flicker in the domain of foreknowledge, filled with a latent joy.

021   White Balls

Why are balls round? Because they have to be—if they were not, ball sports would never have been invented, nor mastery achieved. Applying the same energy twice would produce a different result each time. And so, balls must be round. Technology determines whether a ball can be made round or not. I once saw a ten-thousand-year-old doughnut-shaped stone object with an almost perfectly circular hole in the middle, apparently bored with an implement also made of stone. The hole shows where a hard kind of stone was rotated to cut away a softer one. A perfect circle made without mathematics—just with hands. But a sphere is not so easy. I have seen a photograph of competing German and Japanese technicians with polished glass balls they had tried to make into perfect spheres. They were placing the spheres on thin, smooth tracks to discover how far they would roll on a flat plane. Even today, despite all our sophisticated technology, we cannot completely eliminate all distortions from spheres. Perfection remains strictly an ideal.

From another perspective, a ball's movement embodies the fundamental principles of the universe. Heavenly bodies like the sun and earth are spheres. These huge, spinning masses pull on each other, striking a mutual balance that has determined their shape. The same principle is at work in the balls bouncing about here on earth. Humans may pursue our inquiries ever deeper into the laws of physics, but we feel those principles physically through our ball games. Perhaps we simply desire to confirm our experience. Scientific development improves the precision of balls, which in turn helps ball game athletes improve their performance. Balls are embodied, pliant realizations of the principles of the universe.

Looking at the stitches bulging out of a baseball or the fuzz on a tennis ball, however, one cannot help wondering to what degree those balls are actually precise. In international tennis tournaments, when it's unclear whether a ball is in or out, players now have the right to challenge calls made by line umpires, and view results recorded by three or more high precision cameras. In other words, it is now possible to calculate the exact trajectory of the ball and make a precise judgment one way or the other. A machine's verdict is more reliable than the eyes of a skilled referee. Yet, although we can now measure where it lands, we can't know the exact shape of the ball itself. It is not a perfect sphere, and so even assuming the same momentum, tiny inconsistencies will produce unpredictable results. And since the unstable environment of the grass court is always factored in by observers at the Wimbledon tennis championships, it seems clear that inconsistencies and chance are an inevitable part the game of tennis. It makes for good drama.

Incidentally, conventional wisdom holds that balls should always be white. Yet tennis balls are mainly yellow because, apparently, yellow balls are easier to see. However, by the final rounds of a tournament the grass court, even at Wimbledon, is worn and faded, and the ball's yellow becomes surprisingly dull. How about instituting a rule requiring that just the championship match be played with white balls? I would say that this special white-ball provision—heightening the possibility of precision to the utmost limit—would rather benefit such a momentous event.

022   White Hair and Shaved Heads

I always wear black. I am often asked why, but, in fact, I have no particular reason for it. It is not merely due to laziness. I simply do not find it necessary to drape myself in color or to sport different styles. Wearing the same kind of clothing every day is admittedly rather boring. But I prefer to limit myself to clothing that I feel comfortable in. Perhaps because my job is to design, black is a practical, background color—I am like a stagehand who is meant to provide invisible support to actors during a performance. I suppose I have accepted being "the dyer who wears white," as the saying goes. Or perhaps I wear all black because my hair has gone completely white, and some part of me likes the idea of staking my identity on the contrast between my white hair and black clothes. Since fashion makes art out of life, I suppose I also don these clothes to take life by the horns, hoping the style will help me live life to the fullest.

In the same way, there are those who think that people who wear black do so because they are dark characters, who by their nature inhabit a black atmosphere and would never think to wear colors. There is an organization called AGI—Alliance Graphique Internationale—that has about five hundred members, all designers whose achievements are known across the world. The range of ages within the membership is thus unusually wide. There is an AGI meeting in a different city each year. Besides a general assembly for the members, there is an event called the "AGI Open," which means it is also open to the public. Meeting were held in London in 2013 and São Paulo in 2014. In 2015, while I was preparing this manuscript, one was held in Biel/Bienne, Switzerland, a town known for its watchmaking industry. Since all the members are masterful speakers, the events are surprisingly popular, and the London event, held over two days in the Barbican Centre's main hall (which holds two thousand people) attracted the general public in large numbers. The graphic designers, young and old, were representative of all current styles, and the range of colors they wore at the event was truly striking. Nevertheless, the proportion of black clothing was also very high. Nearly everyone wore either a T-shirt or some other casual garment. Israel's David Tartakover, the United Kingdom's Tony Brook, Germany's Uwe Loesch, who always wears symmetrically opposed black and white shoes, and others—each of these individuals possesses a big personality. Unconcerned with passing fads, they take life at their own pace. A collection of giants—nonetheless, half with shaved heads, half with white hair.

Switzerland's Lars Müller, whose love of books developed into a publishing business, is an eccentric book designer. This barrel-shaped Northern European, with his large black pants and loose black jacket, flits about the world in black shoes and a black backpack with his white hair flying. Once, when I was in a sushi restaurant in Kanazawa with Lars, we were asked, "And what country are you two from?" and I realized then that we are really the same kind of person. We are the black-clothes-wearing, white-haired, and shaved-headed people.

023　Sand

In the eastern part of Indonesia, at the tip of the beak of the condor-shaped island of New Guinea, there is a group of islands called Raja Ampat, which means "the Four Kings." Located where the Pacific and Indian oceans join together, it is said to house the world's richest biodiversity of marine life. The coral reef is especially magnificent. I visited this area in the summer of 2015 to take photographs.

　　Coral is a living organism that inhabits relatively shallow parts of the ocean. The reef scenery resembles a forest or dense jungle, such as you might find on land. We land-dwelling humans have grown accustomed to trees and forests, but we know very little about coral, this entity within the sea, except to see it as a precious, beautiful thing. Yet corals manifest a spectacular diversity of forms. Like all the world's trees, coral is immobile, and yet, as a member of the animal kingdom, it produces eggs. While I was scouting for the photographs, I came to realize that the source of corals' diversity is their proclivity to seek out areas with maximum access to light and water. Corals have evolved to make the most of these natural gifts: they perform photosynthesis and also ingest the plankton in the sea. As a result, their unique evolution has produced a wild and uninhibited growth of fractal shapes reflecting nature's mysterious adaptive force. And yet this force does not default to some predictable, singular form. Round things have complex surface structures. Things that branch out do so in dense formations, forking in every possible direction. Things that swell quickly form countless bumps and protrusions. Petal-like things sprout in multiplicities of identical leaves. Coral is exactly, as the saying goes, "one hundred flowers blooming in profusion simultaneously."

　　One of the more difficult places to get to in the Raja Ampat archipelago is the Waigo Island group—even when the ocean is calm it takes three hours on a high-speed boat to get there from any available lodging. It is an other-worldly place that even the locals rarely visit. The islands jut out of the sea like clusters of mushrooms, rising vertically from the ocean floor in strange formations that result from tectonic changes in the earth's crust; they have also been shaped by the powerful ocean squalls that wash over them continuously. Their surfaces are covered in trees that are somehow reminiscent of bonsai. The superb scenery extends below the water line. Diving in the shallow sea that surrounds the islands, I encountered an awe-inspiring coral reef sprawled across the ocean floor. It took my breath away; it was a stunning example of what the earth would be like without people.

The scenery reminded me of the Sea of Corruption Forest in Miyazaki Hayao's *Nausicaä of the Valley of the Wind*. From the perspective of land-dwelling creatures like us, the forms a coral's life takes may seem surreal or chaotic. Those who study it closely, however, understand that the system that produces the life of coral—a life that stretches over an enormous span of time—is the very definition of natural order. A sea floor of astonishingly white sand surrounded the coral. When I scooped up some in my hand, a smoke-like trail whirled about, then was instantly swept away by the ocean current, and the water once again became crystal clear. The sand was so fine it was impossible to tell its composition. Likely, it consists of minute fragments of the remains of coral and other sea creatures. These tiny fragments —the result of life succeeding life—are bleached by the sun's ultraviolet rays, growing whiter and whiter. The renewal of life and death continually purifies the world. Staring at the sand's whiteness, I could feel my own fundamental relationship with that same rhythm of existence.

024 Laundry

Over a thousand cotton T-shirts hang on a beach, pinned to long clotheslines. They flutter in the breeze, bathed in perpetual sunlight. The view leaves you breathless. These T-shirts make up "The T-Shirt Exhibit" and are part of an art project in Kōchi Prefecture called the Sandy Beach Art Gallery, the brainchild of local designer Umebara Makoto, who says "There is no art gallery in our town. The beach is our art gallery." Rather than bringing in some famous architect for an exorbitant amount of money, and building a pricey "cultural institution," the idea was to explore what it would be like to turn the existing sandy beach into an art gallery.

It is a deserted, gorgeous, white-sand beach. Sometimes whales can be spotted out in the open sea. Next to the beach is a field of Japanese leeks. In late autumn, the field is full of light purple flowers and one can take part in leek flower viewing. There is also a very interesting exhibit in which driftwood from the beach is selected and arranged for viewing. The idea was painstakingly explained to the local municipality, so that everybody understood what it meant for them to turn a beach into an art gallery. The T-shirt exhibition attracted people from all over the world, and the Sandy Beach Art Gallery has assembled an innumerable number of T-shirts printed with illustrations and photographs.

"Wherever the wind takes you" is the catchphrase of the exhibition, and people certainly love it. With the simple image of T-shirts flying like sails in the wind on a plain, empty beach as its basis, the exhibition has been held an incredible twenty-seven times since 1989. To take part, public applicants send in their illustration or design, which is then assigned a particular location within the exhibit. In recent years, the good feelings of its theme, "Wherever the wind takes you," have crossed national borders. Amazingly, the exhibition has been held five times in Mongolia. In 2015, through the gracious support of the JICA—the Japan International Cooperation Agency—it went to Ghana in Africa. Then, in 2016, it also traveled to Kenya.

The spectacle of clean white laundry bathing in the sun and drying in the summer breeze imparts the feeling that the deepest parts of you have also been washed clean and your spirit somehow lifted. Umebara Makoto, the project's originator, says he used a TV commercial for laundry he saw as a boy as reference. There was indeed such a commercial, which aired during Japan's postwar economic miracle. It showed countless pure white T-shirts sparkling in the sunlight as they fluttered in the breeze.

I, too, have a scene in my memory that involves laundry. I am young, clinging to my mother's back in the bright garden behind our home. Water is drip-dropping from a mattress cover just hung out to dry. The wet, glowing cloth brushes my cheek and I wail in discomfort, as I cling to my mother's back. It is a deeply rooted memory—light spilling from a laundered sheet on a clothesline.

025   Silver

Look at silver and you will feel welling up from the deepest recesses of your mind an exhilarating sense of infinite possibility. With light glittering over its highly reflective surface it is an image of luxury like nothing else. Yet, as if to strike a balance, the shadows of tarnish in the intricacies of its design suggest all that is the antithesis of life. But somehow these shadows, too, guide us towards the feeling that we can do anything.

I first became aware of silver in my twenties, when I was wandering about India. I purchased a modest silver bracelet at a street stall. A string of gourd-shaped beads no bigger than grains of rice.... It wasn't a gift for anyone, I bought it for myself because I was spellbound by its refined subtlety—one of silver's defining characteristics. Craftspeople's stalls were lined up along the street. I was captivated by the way these silversmiths managed the light and shadow of the precious material they had been entrusted with.

Silver is mined all around the globe. Once polished, it takes on an elegant white sheen that evokes all kinds of emotions. Unlike iron, it is soft and easy to work with, and has been used in many different cultures to ornament the body. As tableware or cutlery, it tends to signify an exalted social position: unless one has many butlers and attendants to continually maintain its sparkle, silver spoons and forks blacken. Silverware is often ornamented with a three-dimensional carved crest or coat of arms, and these designs carry an inner darkness beneath their shining surface. Shadows lurk behind the rich, lustrous visage.... The royalty and nobility of Europe ate their meals with these impressive utensils, in which light and darkness coexist. The phrase "to be born with a silver spoon in one's mouth" suggests the luxury of having a noble pedigree. Taken to its extreme, however, the phrase also indicates that, perhaps, high birth requires the kind of courage necessary to face the guillotine.

Silver ranks second in the Olympic gold-silver-bronze medal system. Its exchange rate is also inferior to gold. This difference in value is due to the degree of scarcity. Were silver as scarce as gold, it would probably be valued even more highly. In ancient Egypt, silver plating was apparently applied to gold ornaments. Comparing the quality of their luster, we observe that silver shines with greater transparency, brilliance, and purity, as if we were witnessing light itself. The Egyptians must have felt that silver purified the light of the yellow gold.

The world's first currency was issued in Greece. It, too, was silver. The name given to the coin in antiquity was the *drachma*. The word was revived and used for Greek currency in the twentieth century, remaining as the standard unit until Greece entered the European Union and the euro replaced it. Silver has been used for currency throughout the world; this precious metal ensured the exchange of money and goods. In Japan, too, silver money was issued by banks as well as the Ginza silver mint.

Someone once said, "I pour a shot of single malt scotch over a piece of Antarctic ice floating in a Mexican silverware cup, and, while the ice melts under the equatorial sun, I drink." A masterful evocation of silverware's global reach in our lives!

026 Cumulonimbus Clouds

Tomorrow,
White peach. Cicada. Towering summer clouds.

Who first named the cumulonimbus clouds? In Japanese, the word is 入道雲, literally, "the monk cloud." How skillfully named this unique celestial phenomenon is—white clouds rising up in immense masses against the background of blue skies. The word that makes up the name, *nyūdō*, means "monk" or "priest" and must have been chosen because it evokes the peculiar appearance of a monk's shaved head. A truly exciting name for a cloud. It is somewhat similar to the dream-like image of rubbing Aladdin's lamp to come face to face with the genie that emerges from the spout.

The quotation placed before this entry is the concluding lines of a poem by Andō Tsuguo. A friend of mine back in university once recited them to me, and they became stuck somewhere deep inside me like a small bone. I ruminate now and again on this poetic image. When I do, I look up into the distant sky and suddenly feel as if I am inhaling summer air into the depths of my chest. The whiteness of these "towering summer clouds"—billowing high in the blue summer skies as they do—opens a door to some of my distant memories.

The first one is from my elementary school days, soon after the twentieth of July, when summer vacation begins. Our report cards had been given out when classes ended, but I was ignoring mine. In fact, I had not even opened it. Instead, I focused on my great expectations for the rest of the summer. Filled with excitement, I was on my bike, pedaling with all my might towards the prefectural swimming pool. A vinyl bag with the logo of a cosmetics company printed on it dangled from my handlebars. Inside the bag was my bathing suit and towel. I pushed forward single-mindedly in the direction of my bike's shadow, which was cast darkly ahead of me on the paved road. All I wanted was to forget everything and jump into the pool, which had just opened for the summer.

Another memory appears, this one from my high school days. I was waiting to board the ferry that runs between certain islands in the Inland Sea. A rascal friend and I had planned to go camping on those islands as soon as the summer holidays started. So there we were, both wearing stylish, cheap sunglasses, lounging on the wharf. Typically for high school students in Okayama Prefecture at the time, we had taken advantage of the absence of teachers' and parents' watchful eyes, and had hidden imported cigarettes in our shirt pockets—"Western smokes" as we called them. There was still time before the ferry departed, so we sat and gazed at the boats anchored in the harbor. Oysters and corn barnacles clung to a thick rope in the sea. We gazed absentmindedly down at the shadows of fish lazily traversing the sea floor, and I slowly took the plain cigarettes from my pocket and, despite my unfamiliarity with smoking, peeled off the seal. My no-good friend and I lit up. We took quick sidelong looks at each other, both of us completely self-absorbed and obsessed with "having a good time." An embarrassing but endearing episode. I clearly remember the clouds in the distant sky, welling high above the horizon.

I always cheer up under the bright skies of hot summer days. Looking up at the clouds makes me feel I have opened my heart to the summer air—like opening all the windows of a house. I feel this way every summer. No matter where I am on the planet, when I look at those towering clouds, whether from a car or skyscraper window, my thoughts return to those early memories.

027 Waves

I look out over the sea from the window of a passenger plane. The waves cresting on the surface of the sea appear completely still. Waves are formed as the ocean's vast amount of salt water competes with the forces of gravity exerted by the earth and the moon. From up here they look like wrinkles, generated by the fanning of the wind. Those wrinkles break continuously on the shore. The earth—the universe itself—is in constant motion. And so, even during the calmest moments, dynamic activity never ends. Of course, waves do not always break softly against the shore. At times, they become a violent, destructive force that can lay waste to human lives.

Waves are enormous when you are in a boat or standing on the shore. When perceived from an aircraft, even from an altitude of only several hundred meters, however, they seem to move extremely slowly, sometimes appearing to stop altogether. Perhaps this is also due to the speed at which the aircraft is moving. Fixing your unbelieving eyes on the waves will not change this—the waves will still appear frozen in place. I cannot shake off this uncanny sight.

I was once with a group that strayed out into a pitch-black ocean in a tiny outboard motorboat, with not a single light in sight. We had been working on a small island, far removed from any human civilization, directly under the equator. We knew that on calm water it would take the better part of three hours to get back to the mainland, and there was still time before sunset, so we decided to head home. Eight people in one boat. But then the sea started getting rough. Our boat was quick and smooth over a docile, mirror-like sea. But when the sea got rough, every one of those towering waves hit us so hard it felt like we were smashing through walls. Soon it became difficult to make any headway at all. Before long, the sun set. Then in this moonless, starless, jet-black darkness something started to glimmer—phosphorescent sea plankton. The bow of a boat is designed like an edged tool, to cut through the walls of water that strike against it. And yet, the impact of each of these waves was strong enough to make me worry about injuring my back. Ocean squalls descended on us ferociously. The pitch-black night was made even darker by the ocean spray rising around us. Our human sense of direction was so baffled as to be almost worthless. The boat was piloted by a very capable person, but it had neither wireless radio nor GPS. All we could see in its headlights was the surging of the waves, so we shut off the lights. The boat was a tiny black figure in the darkness, pushing forward as best it could. The waves' white crests were not visible, only the enormous black masses glowing with phosphorescent plankton that pounded the boat over and over again.

We endured the pummeling, hunched over in the boat. We ran aground three time in the darkness. Had these been rocky outcrops, we might not have returned alive, for the boat was running at top speed. Luckily, though, we had run into coral and so the boat's hull had not been torn open. When we finally saw the lights of a pearl oyster nursery in the distance, I felt that we had somehow made it home. Going to the island took three hours. Coming back took six.

If you are thrown into the ocean you will be tossed around like a helpless toy. Yet from a distance, the waves appear unmoving. If you look down on the earth from outside the stratosphere, they become entirely invisible. It is said that the earth is blue. Even the roughest waves are still and blue when seen from high above.

028   Waterfalls

There is a massive waterfall system that straddles the border between Argentina and Brazil. It is called the Iguazu Falls. Niagara Falls is large, but the Iguazu Falls appear to be the size of two Niagara-sized falls stacked on each top of other and extending out horizontally four times the width. I visited the location alone to see the falls after finishing up some work in São Paulo. At the invitation of the Japan Foundation, I was on a personal tour exhibiting my work in four North and South American cities—a demanding schedule that took me to Toronto, New York, Guanajuato, and São Paulo. This was in 2001.

If I count the posters I have produced in my career as a graphic designer, it adds up to a very considerable number. Besides posters for commercial clients, I have produced numerous works for exhibitions, international fairs, and even for what you might call social justice. On the 2001 tour, my work was exhibited either in galleries affiliated with the Japan Foundation or at art spaces that the foundation made available for the show. I was also asked to lecture alongside the exhibits.

Posters are easy to display. Each one has its own theme, and the sizes of the images are predetermined—almost like a set of visual *haiku*. The gallery-goers' experience of the work is also straightforward: they are free to enjoy the posters they like best. Even though they are fairly large, posters are simply paper, and so the transportation costs are low. Furthermore, posters are well suited to framing.

I sent approximately seventy posters to each of the four cities. When I arrived I took a look at the display, arranging and straightening the frames; I appeared at one lonesome exhibit and lecture after another. What kept me company on this solitary trip was the critic Kobayashi Hideo's *Collected Lectures*, which I carried around with me on my MiniDisc player. I would sit in an airport just before dawn, or in a hotel in Mexico—a country I had never visited before—listening to Kobayashi's voice, which always sounded like he was chewing on dried squid, reading his essays on the eighteenth-century scholar Motoori Norinaga or on Norinaga's poem "Mountain Cherry Tree."

To visit the Iguazu Falls, you must take an airplane from São Paulo. During the flight, I worried that the reports of their grandeur might have been exaggerated. But I remembered the words of the great veteran designer, Awazu Kiyoshi: "It is always better to get out and see for yourself the wonders of nature—its waterfalls, deserts, and the like." I have heeded this advice as much as possible ever since. I have come to understand that you get something from each trip.

In the language of the region, Iguazu means "big water." You walk along a boardwalk surrounded by thick trees and then, suddenly, a white wall of water appears right before your eyes. The central part of the waterfall system, covered in a misty haze, is called "the Devil's Throat" with a drop of eighty meters. In one spot, you can see the water falling directly in front of you. As this overwhelming mass of water, an entity far beyond any human ingenuity, crashed down directly before me, I began to feel sick. Several times higher than a skyscraper, this impossibly large, unendingly speeding mass was so close I could reach out and touch it. In comparison, humans seemed smaller than ants. It made me dizzy—it felt as though I was suffering from motion sickness. My human scale, the scale my senses work at, was blown apart by earth's incredible gravity, its surging waves. My exhibition tour also disappeared into the white, raging tumult.

029 Fingers

My heart beats faster whenever I see beautiful fingers. I, of course, also enjoy their movements and gestures, but I am mostly fascinated by the shape of the fingers themselves. Slim, tidy fingers with long—but not too long—unadorned fingernails. When I see such fingers, I enter a state of—what would you call it—erotic delight? Passionate arousal? I find myself struck by their refined existence—the way they exude intelligence, or the way they signify how well their owners take care of their bodies. "Hands are the brains of the external body"—I remember hearing this phrase somewhere. Hands are indeed a special sense organ. We move our hands as we think of things; we feel the world. I find the shape of fingers as unique sense organs of touch to be truly amazing.

The hand of the woman in Leonardo da Vinci's *Lady with an Ermine* is a particularly splendid example from the world of painting. There is something about that hand that rivets me. The woman herself is charming: she is young, with a curious hair style, her fine hair arranged neatly and tucked under her chin. Her soft features, the exquisite curve of her cheek and the shape of her closed mouth naturally draw my attention. At the same time, I truly cannot take my eyes off the white hand holding the ermine. You can feel the veins under her pale skin. From the way the fingers spread outward, and the shape of her fingernails, you feel that you know the life she leads in her secluded room, her personality, everything about soul and her ultimate fate. And what is this slender, beautiful hand offering up? Not a black cat. Not a curly-haired golden puppy. But an ermine—a white-coated stoat—a wild, potentially ferocious animal.

The expressive qualities of the fingers we see in Japan's *uki-yo-e* woodblock prints are also quite distinctive. This is especially true of Utamaro's series called "Large-Headed Pictures of Beautiful

Women"—*Bijin-ga Ōkubi-e*—where the hands of women depicted in close-up are particularly exquisite. The one I like best is titled *Uwaki no Sō* ("the flighty type"). With her breast exposed, holding a towel, she has a faraway look. Perhaps she has her eyes on a handsome man. Or someone else she admires. Either way, her distracted expression is pleasing. Perhaps because she is preoccupied with someone off in the distance, she seems to have forgotten about her hands. I find this to be extremely charming.

The style of depicting fingers in ukiyo-e is unique. Of course, not every woman living in Edo clipped her nails as short as possible. Yet the fingertips in these ukiyo-e are so plump that the short nails almost disappear. Who popularized this image? It exemplifies an expression that was used for long, slender fingers—literally, "whitebait-like fingers"—white fingers with a rounded aesthetic. Fingers whose skin is taut as though from some pressure within.

They remind me of a particular moment in high school. I was attempting to dress up as a Playboy Bunny for my school's activity day and some of my female classmates were helping me apply makeup. They patted white coverup on my face and did my fingernails to make my fingers look dainty and thin. It was the first time I experienced the touch of the opposite sex on my face.

030   The Nape of the Neck

Have you heard of "Kaze no Bon"—the Bon Festival of the Wind? It is held in Yatsuo, Toyama Prefecture, each year for three days starting from the first day of September. A dance is performed at this festival, a dance that expresses what one might call a dignified, refined flirtatiousness. The young male and female dancers convey through their movements the distinctive charms of masculinity and femininity, to the accompaniment of a regional folk song, the sorrowful "Ecchu Owara Bushi." For some reason the instrument that plays the melody—the *kokyū*—comes from China, a foreign country. Its painful tone heralds the fall of night as the musicians lead groups of dancers through the town. There is a sense of quiet, mysterious excitement.

My reason for visiting Yatsuo was unrelated to Kaze no Bon. This was in 1995, and I was there to visit Yoshida Keisuku, the eighty-year-old manager of a Japanese paper-making—or *washi*—company called Keijusha. In those days, I was trying to establish a centre for the research and preservation of traditional washi in Aoya, Tottori Prefecture, a region known for producing such paper. Although I was doing all I could to push the project forward, an elder of the region, Shio Yoshiro, was opposed to it. He stubbornly refused to give me his permission no matter how hard I tried to persuade him. Today, washi production has declined so much it can no longer be called an industry. Its future is in doubt. At the time, though, I believed that such paper could find its place among tomorrow's successful products, and that Aoya's young washi-makers were the key. So I went to Toyama to visit Yoshida Keisuku. He was the right person to talk to because he knew Shio Yoshiro from the Folk Art Movement of Yanagi Sōetsu and Serizawa Keisuke. When I presented Mr. Yoshida with my publications and plans, he tried to be supportive, but it was clear that Shio's influence was too great. I felt defeated, as if I should just forget everything, as if some evil spirit had infiltrated my body. I had feared the washi project would not work out, yet the fact that my feelings had been justified gave me no satisfaction. On the contrary, it made me painfully aware of what seemed like my own failure. Maybe I should scrap my plan and start over. That night, Yoshida Keisuku let me sleep in his private studio, which was set apart from his main house. It was a strange and wonderful museum-like space, with folk art he had collected from around the world displayed on the walls and shelves.

That night was Kaze no Bon. I strolled the town alone and watched the Owara dancers—organized by a local institution—moving through the streets. There are two styles of dancing, one for men and one for women. The women wear straw-braided hats folded in half low over their eyes—so low that their faces are almost entirely concealed. Correspondingly, the hair is swept up, leaving the bare nape of their neck exposed. This is not the sly, wide open nape of a geisha. Bound by the hat's red strings, the ears and the back of the neck, as well as part of the cheek and jaw, peek out demurely from under the hat. Done up this way, each and every participant somehow appears to be an exquisite beauty. I was struck by a deep admiration when I told Yoshida Keisuku of my impression. He said, looking very satisfied, "That's Yatsuo's aesthetic!" Aesthetic…. It sounded great right then.

I was completely bowled over by the white nape of the neck of a woman I did not even know! I guess falling for a woman you cannot identify cannot be called love, but that burning image entranced me for some time.

Even now, as the fall wind blows, I can feel my heart pounding as that white nape below the red strings of the hat rises to my mind once again.

031 Amateur

Akita Prefecture's Tsuru-no-yu Onsen in Nyūtō, on the shore of Tazawako lake, is one of Japan's most popular hot-springs *ryokan*. The cloudy-white, open-air bath at the inn is particularly enjoyable, and, despite the presence of both sexes, even young and attractive women join in. The bath's beautiful surroundings seem to overcome their typical opposition to mixed bathing. In winter the bath is covered in snow; in summer it is concealed by summer grasses. Ancient thatched houses, with their sunken floor hearths, have been moved to this area and rebuilt. Enter one and your heart melts. Picture yourself drinking Akita's local sake with a group of smiling friends while indulging in delicious Japanese mountain yam nabe from a pot hanging from a hook—absolute bliss.

The proprietor, Satō Kazushi, once asked me for a favor, namely to design a handbag for a ceremony commemorating the forty-year anniversary of the Japan Association of Secluded Hot Spring Inns, the Tsuru-no-yu Onsen being one of its affiliates. One can easily imagine being asked to design a hand towel, but this time it was a handbag. Satō specifically wanted handbags so that the members of the association could take them home along with sake as souvenirs after the ceremony. This was something of a delicate job, but I could not say no to the Association. I agreed to Satō's request.

After some thought, I decided to try my hand at writing the *hiragana* character *yu*—which means "hot water," and refers to onsen. Now, I am only an amateur calligrapher, though I have some experience designing characters for fonts or logotypes. My mother practices calligraphy, but I hate strict teachers telling me what to do, so I have steered clear of the brushes since I was a child. Then I thought, "What if I use that amateur quality to my advantage?"

Returning to my parents' house in Okayama, I borrowed my mother's studio space and earnestly began writing "*yu*." I wrote out variation after variation, drawing my inspiration from a font dictionary. Writing with ink and a brush is very different from drawing a picture. The especially strange thing about a calligrapher's light black ink is that the line you initially write appears to float over the lines you add afterwards. This exercise was quite unusual for me, but I decided to cast aside any concern that I was unskilled or would produce something of poor quality. Instead, I told myself that I was the first person to write in such a unique way, and I began to write in lively, bold strokes. An expert calligrapher may do this to avoid making their skill too obvious, but this was simply the calligraphy of an unapologetic amateur.

I selected about a dozen iterations of *yu* from the vast assortment I had created and mounted them on paper. Then, I affixed them to both sides of a handbag above a secret *onsen* scene taken from my imagination. The seal of the Japan Association of Secluded Hot Spring Inns was commissioned and carved by a skilled engraver from Suzhou, China. I pressed this seal into a soft red inkpad and applied it to the handbag. Seeing this seal amongst my noisy "*yu*" calligraphy produced a wonderfully striking tension.

I showed the finished bag to the Kōchi Prefecture-born designer Umebara Makoto, and surprisingly, it elicited a rare word of praise. "You nailed it," was his brief comment. Umebara and I are onsen travel buddies, so he is a reliable source for onsen aesthetics. I must say, though, that this job was a departure from my usual style. Perhaps it would have been more suited to Umebara's skill set as a minimalist designer. Perhaps that was why his single compliment resonated with the force of a thousand. It occurred to me that one of the charms of white is that it is the absolute antithesis of black—the thought made me feel a little conceited. But I could not let it go to my head. When dealing with the Association, I was necessarily an amateur. I knew I should never lose sight of that fact.

032 Plain Hot Drinking Water

Tea is drunk all over the world. And yet, Japan appears to be the only place where people drink plain boiled water, a drink given the lofty name of, literally, "white, hot water."

In Japanese, the term *kaiseki ryōri* or "chest-stone cooking" refers to the food served during tea gatherings. The name is apparently derived from the story of a Zen priest who staved off his hunger by slipping a heated stone inside his kimono. Essentially, the term suggests a modest, frugal meal. However, the dishes served at a present-day tea gathering—called *chaji*—are focused not on modesty but rather on comfort and abundance. Chosen to reflect the season, the food is served according to a meticulous plan that dictates not only the ingredients but also the vessels it is served in. The gathering is designed to enhance the daily ins and outs of life—the drinking of tea, the taking of nourishment—and to supplement these activities with a sense of beauty.

Before entering the tea room, the guests are offered plain hot drinking water, not green tea and not sake. As one drinks it, one feels one's mind and body being cleansed of the soiling effect of everyday life. The characters for "plain hot water"—white, *sa*; hot water, *yu*—are indeed beautiful, but the sound *sayu* is beautiful, too. We hear a similar sound, *sayo*, literally small (*sa*) and night, *yo*, in the word for "evening." A small night, *sayo*; white, boiled water, *sayu*—these delicate alterations of sound mark a consciousness that works to enrich a monotone world with poetic intonations. Perhaps this activity is what defines Japanese culture. I have always enjoyed playing with these subtle qualities of beauty.

And so, I decided to try to design a vessel especially for this "white, hot water." You can neither transmit nor revive traditions simply by intellectually comprehending them. I believe you have to get your hands dirty and test solutions for yourself, if you hope to truly understand something. I have no experience in making ceramics, and I am truly hopeless when it comes to kneading clay or turning a potter's wheel, so I decided to approach the problem the only way I know how—through industrial manufacturing design. I made a rough shape out of papier-mâché and, after it dried, used sandpaper to work it into the precise shape I wanted. I then produced a drawn outline using this shape as the model.

I used a Joseon *hakuji* "water drop" teapot I had on hand as a reference. These are small teapots with a full, round bulge at the top. I considered the tautness of its curved surface. It gives the feeling that there is some force inside the pot causing it to bulge in this way. I did not include a handle as I wanted to maintain the pouring method common to such smooth, rounded small teapots, which one grasps with a cloth to protect against the heat of the boiled water. For the actual manufacturing of the vessel, I commissioned a Jingdezhen *hakuji* workshop that I have grown close to. We used a pottery stone known to produce extremely white porcelain. I decided to also commission two teacups.

For the finishing touches I placed the set in a Chinese-style wooden box. Unlike the paulownia boxes, this kind has a lid that you pull off. The thick, cushion-like buffer that lines the inside ensures all the pieces fit snugly in place. The end result was surprisingly good, probably thanks to a friend of mine, a Chinese Zen priest who acted as a go-between during the production process. I immediately named the set "Drinking Set for Plain Hot Water," wrote down its origin on a piece of deckle-edged Japanese paper and pasted the paper to the box. Of course, I partake of some plain boiled water with the teapot from time to time, but I also enjoy it simply for what it is—an embodiment of *sayu*.

033 White Gowns

Doctors and scientific researchers alike wear white gowns. The gowns are collared, long-sleeved, and knee-length. They are not really uniforms, but they are almost always worn—why? Well, medical examinations and chemistry experiments require an appropriately serious costume. Showy, patterned clothing in such situations just would not look right. The atmosphere of a place changes when someone puts on a white gown. It helps both the person administering a medical exam and the person receiving it to feel calm.

The question remains, why white gowns, specifically? Viewed objectively, an unbleached, muted color or a respectful black or indigo would surely work just as well. Yet the gowns in question are not even a vague, unbleached white, but are such a fastidious, bright white they almost hurt your eyes. Perhaps the whiteness forces the wearer to take pains to stay as clean as possible. It takes courage to wear "that which is easily dirtied"—so easily dirtied, in fact, that even the most minuscule speck of grime is visible at a glance. The effort it takes to preserve this state of extreme cleanliness is perhaps a tacit acknowledgement that clinics, hospitals, and laboratories, by their nature, can be rather tense places.

Injuries and sudden illnesses can cause anxiety and require medical procedures that involve a race against time. Yet, paradoxically, when there is an appropriate level of tension in the air, one feels more at ease than if the place was too relaxed, too calm. This must be why such a high level of cleanliness is demanded. For doctors, having your gown stained by blood or medicine is just part of the job. By changing immediately and keeping their white gowns spotless, therefore, they can give people the impression that the hospital is carefully managed. I expect this is essentially the same reason why bandages and gauze are white. One could say, too, that the unblemished whiteness of these dressings, designed so that that wounds do not become recontaminated, is also a signal that the hospital is being run in a rigorous way.

Tablecloths at top restaurants are also snow white. Again, this is done as a sign of the restaurant's state of cleanliness, not just in pursuit of elegance. If a lavish ostentatiousness were the aim, then surely using a gorgeously colored tablecloth would be more effective. And if hiding wine stains was their goal, a dark red would make more sense. Yet, by using a pure white cloth, the restaurant implicitly suggests to the customers that their table is impeccably clean. This seems to rate higher on the list of service priorities than showy decoration. I think white napkins and a chef's white clothes follow the same principle.

Incidentally, for some reason more people are wearing white masks these days in Japan. Has this everyday mask-wearing been triggered by pollen allergies? This increase has unwittingly led to a certain tension in our day-to-day environments. It makes me feel uncomfortable. I understand wearing a mask if one has caught a cold and wants to prevent its spread or protect one's throat. That a doctor would want to wear a mask during surgery is, of course, completely reasonable. Yet it is somehow ominous when the staff at arrival and departure counters in airports or at convenience stores wear masks. Do they not realize that covering their faces with white has a powerful effect on those they are speaking with? It is like looking at a Noh mask—it cancels any sense of familiarity, however small.

034 Flesh-Colored

I came across a box of eye-popping, bright-blue adhesive bandages at a drugstore in London. One expects this kind of product to conform to the various colors of skin, so these blue ones seemed somehow dubious. Thinking they would make a good talking point, I bought them. And yet, my doubts gradually melted away as I gazed at my own hands. In a word, London is a melting pot of ethnic groups: the people living there are of many different skin colors—white, yellow, black. From nearly transparent white to reddish brown, from chocolate brown to as black as a morning glory seed—the differences are both subtle and dramatic. The middle-of-the-spectrum, "flesh-colored" varieties of adhesive bandages sold in Japan simply would not suffice. What I feel compelled to call the extraterrestrial deep blue of these bandages is perhaps its own "middle-of-the-spectrum." My half-forgotten prejudice, based on the beige crayon called "flesh-colored" in the twelve-crayon set I played with as a child, was thankfully shattered by my experience in that London drugstore.

When you think about it, skin color is quite variable. Skin is also semi-transparent to varying degrees, so that in some cases the flesh, fat, or blood vessels show through. Skin is also three-dimensional; it has depth. The level of transparency is completely different between, say, skin with a lot of fat underneath it and dry skin. This transparency also differs depending on the state of blood circulation. It is extremely changeable, as when some people's skin turns red when they drink alcohol.

Skin's appearance also changes with age. A baby's skin is delicate, and its chubby arms, legs, and face—which seem to glow from within—all appear to be the same color. Perhaps the original notion of "flesh-colored" derives from this. But although young skin appears to be uniform, it becomes increasingly inconsistent as one ages. Veins appear on its surface. Wrinkles, dullness, and spots begin to stand out. As these changes occur, skin's appearance is completely altered. Just as the texture of tree bark alters dramatically as a tree grows from a sapling into a forest giant, human skin acquires an air of consequence and dignity as one ages.

It might be fun to develop a grid-like matrix, arranging the colors of adhesive bandages in accordance with age and ethnicity. Imagine it: an array of colors spreading out vertically and horizontally, so that for every ten levels of gradation there are one hundred different skin tones. This would be a far more truthful representation of "flesh-colored" tones. Indeed, some bandages have recently taken on a semi-transparency not unlike skin, conforming more closely to a wider variety of colors than before. I also hear talk of bandages that would change color to match the surrounding skin tone when applied, but that plan seems not to have come to fruition yet.

On the other hand, surgical dressings and gauze pads are usually white. Is this because the pads are applied to unseen areas of the body? Such pads seem to be taking huge leaps both in terms of technology and physical make-up—some are high-tech fibrous types that elastically stretch and contract in compliance with the movements of the muscles; others optimize the balance between adhesive strength and ease of removal. These easily applied, intensely white pads seem to exude effectiveness. If such aids were designed for space aliens, a whiter-than-white shade might in fact be that middle-of-the-spectrum flesh color.

035 Tabi

How feet are handled is an integral part of any culture. In Japan, not entering a home with one's shoes on, making sure to take any footwear off at the *genkan*, carries a symbolic meaning. The piece of wood supporting the step at the *genkan* threshold—the *agarika-machi*—is not there, in other words, simply to protect against mud or dust. Rather, the difference in elevation is ceremonial; it prevents even invisible impurities from being tracked in. There are scenes in historical plays where characters wash their feet at this wooden step. *Zōri* or *waraji* sandals do get dirty, no matter how carefully you walk —it's unavoidable. That is why the characters are sure to wash their feet before going indoors. In Japanese, the phrase "to wash one's feet" also means to shun shady business practices and turn towards honest ones. To cleanse oneself of all impurities. It is, so to speak, a rite of purification.

White *tabi*—Japanese split-toed socks—symbolize clean feet that have passed through such a purification ritual. We wear these socks in ceremonial spaces indoors. They are a sign that one has taken the necessary steps to clean and prepare one's feet. Like the *agarikama-chi* they are not simply functional; we wear them as symbols of purity.

Tabi are tailored from cloth that completely lacks flexibility. This requires that the cloth be worked into the shape of a foot before-hand. You put them on by inserting your foot into this pre-shaped form. They are arranged so that the big toe is separated from the other four. Clasps at the back secure the tabi to your foot. These qualities make the sensation of wearing them entirely different from that of socks made with flexible material. Such elastic materials fit snugly to the body, revealing its contours. Both kimono and tabi, however, are designed to conceal the human form. Inherent in their design is an aesthetic sense that favors a predetermined style. A kimono is tailored from a single bolt of cloth. Its shape thus emerges from the form of the cloth as it surrounds the body, which hides the physical shape within. The sensibility at play here aims not only to limit the exposure of skin, but also to define the way the shape of the body itself is presented.

Perhaps the best way to keep your balance and stand firm is to spread all five toes wide as if to grip the earth. One could extend this metaphorically to suggest that if you want to steady your behavior and attitude, you must steady your feet first. Japanese footwear is centered on the space between the big and index toes, which pinch the sandal strap inserted between them. *Geta*, *zōri*, the leather-soled *zōri*, and many other traditional shoes are worn in this way.

I sometimes wear tabi when taking part in strenuous physical activities. I remember putting on a pair to protect a foot I had injured during kendo fencing, when the skin on the foot started peeling away. I always chose black or deep blue tabi that matched the color of the training clothes I was wearing or the equipment I used. The wooden floor of the dojo was slippery, so I would soak a dust cloth in water and step on it in my tabi to make them sticky.

I also slip on a pair when I enter a tea-ceremony room. If I don't I can't relax. Even if my socks are spotless, I feel uncomfortable without that symbol of purity. The tabi may be somewhat stiff, but that secure sense of settling into their forms is, paradoxically, pleasant. Such a feeling is well suited to the *fusuma* and *shōji* of the tea house.

036 Nakedness

There is something uniquely human in the way we perceive "nakedness." Other animals experience no such thing. Hair protects their bodies from external injuries and regulates their temperature. When humans first began walking upright our hands were freed. In almost no time, we began producing fabrics to cover our bodies, and clothes were born. In the beginning, we used the skin and hair of beasts. And then thread was invented. We wove and knitted this thread into increasingly elaborate garments, and as technology advanced, clothing became more and more sophisticated. Clothing makes it possible for humans to survive in the most frigid regions of the earth and will eventually protect us from even the vacuum of space. Body hair gradually disappeared during this process so that all we have left are a few spots of modest hair and a soft, downy fuzz covering the surface of our skin. To be naked is to be utterly defenseless. Such a state—lacking even a single strip of cloth—is now thought of as quite peculiar.

Beyond their basic protective function, clothes have come to symbolize social position or ideology. Uniforms are a form of signification, clearly displaying membership in a group, or proclaiming a particular viewpoint. Clothing excels at making these things obvious, and not just to others; a uniform also influences the wearer, affecting our mentality when we put it on. I am deeply interested in the way that the socially expected behavior implied by one's clothes takes over one's inner self, as if we had become possessed by a costume. If one self-identifies as a chef, then that identity becomes all the more pronounced, it seems, when one is clad in chef's whites. The same holds true in a plane, with the uniform of a cabin crew member. I believe very specific patterns of behavior emerge from the way both the viewer and wearer experience the uniform. When a baseball player puts on a uniform, especially one that carries the number of a star player, both audience and player become co-owners of the fantasies of their respective roles. Lamentably, we can assume the same effect holds true when combat uniforms are involved.

According to the world of fashion, clothing is a clear form of expression. Through fashion, one can either stand out from or blend into one's surroundings. Either way, people are covered in meaning. Our clothes are our informational armor, a function that has long since gone past mere protection. Given the symbols and significance of clothing, nakedness is indeed felt as a peculiar projection of empty space —the space that clothes usually occupy. The shock value of "streaking," or running naked in public view, is not due to any sexual significance. Rather, it is produced by a gap in meaning, by the realization that our original, natural body can appear so bizarre.

I recently worked on the design of a wonderful book, a collection of Utamaro's *bijinga*—prints of beautiful women—and *shunga* —prints of erotic scenes. Once again, I felt overwhelmed by the charm and intensity of the pale-white body parts peeking out from the folds of the kimono. I am well aware that the color of naked skin in the images is simply the white paper used for woodblock printing. Yet this skin, the public exposure of which was prohibited at the time Utamaro made his prints, leaves a much whiter impression than the color of the paper. Something inside us escapes when a kimono opens—something surges forth when skin is exposed—something from the realm of instinct.

037 Yukata

The *yukata* is a garment linked to the pleasure we take when we bathe in a hot spring, not only the simple physical enjoyment but also the otherworldly feeling that our bodies have been purified in some magical way. You unfold a yukata, which is usually stiff from starch, as though untangling it. Flinging it open behind your back, you slide your arms into the sleeves. At that moment your body passes from this world to that other world—the world of hot water. You quickly tie up the *obi* and breathe a sigh of relief. Already you have been liberated from earthly desires and the woes of humankind.... Your feet naturally lead you towards the awaiting steam.

The yukata is designed to be easy to change into and out of. Tug lightly on that slick obi and the garment gently slips away. Today, some people wear underwear underneath their yukata, a most unrefined practice. The yukata is a type of kimono designed specifically to be worn over nothing but one's naked skin. You remove the yukata—or rather, allow it to slip off your body, lightly fold it, and toss it into your change-room basket before heading excitedly towards the bath with nothing but a small towel.

Japan is a country full of hot springs. You can find thermal springs the world over, so the phenomenon tends to be misunderstood as something unremarkable, something that you could encounter in any country. But this is not the case. Survey the world and you'll see that only in Iceland and Japan can you find such a sheer abundance of hot spring water gushing out of the earth. In other words, such countries are rare. Japan is an archipelago isolated by the ocean that stretches toward the eastern edge of Eurasia. It is topographically unique, covered in densely forested mountains that lie along an active fault line, and many, even today, are "volcanoes"—"fire mountains" in Japanese—still in the midst of their mountain-making tectonics.

This country of steep mountains is long from north to south and narrow from east to west. It thus possesses a myriad of subtle seasonal shifts. For each season there are seasonal foods. Every facet of our culture exhibits a delicate sensibility that seeks to determine what are seasonally ideal ingredients. Naturally, this sensibility is manifested when we delight in hot springs. Our baths are arranged in open-air settings so cleverly constructed that you could be forgiven for thinking the hot water gushing out of their rocky walls is entirely natural. This has engendered a style unlike any other in the world. The rock used in the baths, for example, wears down in such a way that it feels just right against the skin. This exquisite smoothness—the result of countless people reclining against the rocks' surface—affords a quiet sense of comfort, as if you were cuddling with an old cat. Soaking in these outdoor rock baths, however, is not an expensive pleasure available only to the rich. Rather, it is a quiet, humble happiness given to us by nature. Leaning against these rocks puts you at ease. A blissful self-forgetting makes you feel truly happy to be alive....

And what is it that graciously ushers you into that other world? The yukata. The Japanese parts of my body feel somehow restrained as I move about in Western clothing. But when I drape a yukata over that body, I feel like a werewolf with the full moon in my eyes—I suddenly change into a totally Japanese person. The starched cotton against my skin liberates me. I feel I have abandoned everything but my naked body. Now then! No need to rush—gently fling that small white towel over your shoulder!

038 Iceland

Despite its frigid-sounding name, Iceland is not really all that cold. Greenland, the country's neighbor, sounds much warmer, but in fact is colder. Thanks to the warm currents that flow through its part of the ocean, Iceland is warmer than even Finland and Sweden, despite occupying the same latitude. Everywhere you go, and I speak from first-hand experience, you can see thermal water flowing from the earth and steam rising into the air. Iceland is situated on an underwater ridge produced by colliding tectonic plates, and has slowly worked its way up from its subterranean origins. Observation posts across the country report the land is pulling apart, a few centimeters a year, one half going east and the other west. Like Japan, Iceland is a volcanic country. Occasionally these volcanoes erupt with such explosive force that, as in 2010, their smoke and ash can throw air traffic over the European continent into chaos.

Iceland's topography—a mass of projections rising from the ocean floor as a result of those mountain-making tectonics—is extremely rugged, seemingly unchanged from the time it was pushed up from the sub-oceanic mantle. There are cliffs everywhere, each seeming to have its own flowing waterfall. The country's charm is crystallized in this majestic scenery, in landscapes that seem to embody nature's dynamism in an unaltered state.

Iceland is about as large as the islands of Hokkaido and Shikoku put together. Rich fishing grounds produced by the collision of warm and cold ocean currents surrounding the country have sustained the Icelandic people since ancient times. The country recently had a thriving financial sector, prior to the bankruptcy of Lehman Brothers, but the global financial crisis left deep scars. Since then, the economy has attained a delicate equilibrium, stabilized by its fishing industry. This balance is in part also the result of reconsidering the male-centric, speculative business management model the country used to rely on, and improving women's social position and influence. The population is small, but the country is thus also spacious and calm. Its people, like the Japanese, live a long time. Unlike Japan, however, perhaps due to its population size, there is almost no difference between the life expectancy of men and women.

The capital city, Reykjavik, has the largest open-air bath in the world—the Blue Lagoon. Almost 30 percent of Iceland's electric power is produced by geothermal energy. Geothermal power plants spew out unending clouds of steam as their turbines churn from the pressure shooting out from underground. And the boiling water that gushes out with the vapor is reused as the Blue Lagoon's water. The rugged, lava-rock bottom has been slowly worn down to make a smooth surface. The onsen's size?—almost exactly that of a baseball stadium, so enormous that only the heaviest hitter could manage a home run. And yet this giant space is filled with hot, blue-tinged, milky-white water. The view is breathtaking. Even if onsen is not your thing, it's hard to stand and look at this scene without wanting to jump in.

The water gushing from the ground contains high levels of silica. This mineral, which is used in the production of latex, gives the water its blue-white color. If you thrust your hand down to the onsen floor, you can scoop up soft white mud. People smear the mud over their hands and face as they bathe believing that it will give them beautiful skin. The water is waist-deep and relatively tepid. There is a bar set up on an artificial bank, so people can enjoy an alcoholic drink while they enjoy the water. Dotted across the bluish-white water are extremely fair-skinned Icelandic people typical of the Scandinavian region. This onsen, as one would expect, has an emotional atmosphere quite different from Japan's. Of course, Iceland is covered in snow during the winter. The snow-covered Blue Lagoon must also be gorgeous.

039 Cotton and Peroxide

A generation ago, there was no problem if a child took a tumble. Children ran, and fell. They skated—slipped and fell. Played baseball —fell. Sumo wrestling, fighting, playing dodgeball, athletic meets, cultural festivals—children fell down. Jungle gyms and slides were also made without much care; they were part of playgrounds that looked more like construction sites or vacant lots, places today's parents would surely reject out of hand as too dangerous. I remember my hands were often pricked and stabbed by thorns, my knees covered in nearly healed scabs. We would calmly pick up praying mantises and stag beetles; we learned how ferocious insects can be, as they stung us and bit us. And yet we kept trying to catch them. We pushed through forests and thickets, accumulating scratches as we went. Small injuries were an everyday occurrence. In that way, you must admit, we actively and directly experienced the world through play. Today, children in developed countries lack even the tiniest scratch or bruise. They have never even scraped a knee. Instead, they have grown up in rooms that are strangely sterile. This is not limited to Japanese children. I have recently felt the same vibe from the children of well-off Chinese families.

We owed everything to our first-aid kits in those times of small injuries. Inside you would always find at the ready a bottle of hydrogen peroxide and, something you do not see so often these days, merbromin (also known as mercurochrome). There were bottles filled with small pieces of gauze soaked in the yellow antiseptic Rivanol. There was sterilized cotton, protective gauze bandages, dark brown adhesive plaster, and even tweezers and scissors. Peroxide is a transparent fluid used to disinfect wounds. One soaks a piece of white cotton with it and, with tweezers, presses the cotton against the infected area. This operation covers the wound with a light, white foam. The more foam, the more the spot stings. I was told this was the peroxide doing its job, though, so I tolerated the pain as best I could.

The peroxide was applied several times until the bubbles finally stopped, whereupon you would cover the wound in merbromin as a final precaution. The merbromin-applied area would turn bright red. The color was oddly conspicuous, as if to prove the injury was real. If the wound was not too large, your treatment was now done. But with more serious wounds, you would patch up the area with the yellow antiseptic Rivanol-soaked gauze, slap on a stretch of clean gauze, and finish it off with an adhesive plaster.

I received this medical treatment exclusively from either my mother or the school nurse. I will never forget the way I felt when my cuts and scratches were treated, and I watched the yellow antiseptic seep into the gauze. Thinking back, I remember that the foaming peroxide, gauze and white bandages made me feel safe and calm. Incurring these injuries, and being treated for them, was crucial to growing up. The overly cautious, scratch-and-bruise-preventing environments of today, and yesterday's skillfully applied, even elegant bandages represent two very different times.

040 Mathematics

The word "mathematics" in Japanese is a translation of the English word, which comes from the Greek *mathemata* (that which should be learned). The original scope of mathematics was apparently much more extensive than what we now understand of the discipline. According to the author of *The Mathematical Body*, Morita Masao, mathematics works to "improve our understanding of what we already know." This is an interpretation of what Martin Heidegger called "learning," his notion that "to learn is to reexamine once again what one has already, implicitly, come to know." Morita claims that this is essentially true for mathematics as well.

Indeed, from the moment we are born into this world, human beings instinctively negotiate the physical environment. If I pay attention, I notice I am carrying out the action of "standing." I unconsciously perform "seeing." Without understanding the reasons, I practice "comparing." I am not calculating the pull of gravity or the firmness of the floor when I stand. Nor am I consciously moving my retina in accordance with my understanding of the principles of light to see. The body comprehends these principles of the universe in some way that has nothing to do with reason. In other words, "living" exists before our recognition of it. Thus, to study physics or mathematics is to reexamine through reason what the body already knows.

Mathematics is not a system of scientific knowledge about those abstractions called "numbers." Instead, it is a continuous fumbling around with the rules of the universe, rules that govern us, too, as living creatures. My body, thrown into the world at birth, is really a mass of questions. The urge to understand mathematics must derive from our feeling that the universe resonates with our bodies and our intuition.

I grapple with the world through that set of ideas called "design." Morita Masao once asked me, "Isn't design mathematics without numerical formulas?" Humans, cast into the world, observe our environment through our various faculties. A designer's basic outlook might be summed up in the question: *How can we change our environment? Have we improved or added to civilization?* The mathematician also speculates about what kind of tools or objects we can use to deepen our understanding of the world. Perhaps design and mathematics share a single origin.

If we think of *shiroshi*—whiteness—as a state of full awareness in striking contrast to the darkness of ignorance, then mathematics in that sense is also white. The chaos and disorder of undifferentiated experience was called *itoshiroshiki* (or *ichijirushiki*) in ancient Japanese, and shiroshi might also be characterized as the light of recognition that rises out of that chaos.

Incidentally, I hear that "prime numbers" are popular among mathematicians—i.e. numbers that can only be divided by either 1 or themselves. Apparently, to young academics visiting the public bath, the shoe storage boxes appear covered in prime numbers—2, 3, 5, 7, 11, 13, 17, and so on. *Prime number*—what a perfectly apt phrase. But I wonder how the mathematics community feels about it.

041 Formulas and Chalk

Telling you about my preference for writing with chalk on a blackboard might make me sound old-fashioned, but I am convinced that mental activities deeply correspond with physical ones. This is especially true of the act of writing. Most of us have become so reliant on keyboards to write out words for us that we never think of such things as chalk or pencils. But even the most advanced, cutting-edge mathematics still favors blackboards. I was deeply impressed when I heard this.

This story starts with chalk. It is about the Japanese manufacturing company, Hagoromo Stationery, which closed its doors in March 2015. For more than eighty years the company had produced chalk that possessed some unique characteristics—it wrote smoothly, it was difficult to break, and the powder didn't smudge your hands. Within Japan it was known as the "Rolls-Royce of the chalk world" and the product was so well-liked this accolade even spread abroad. In short, it was a very popular brand. It seems that its tragic disappearance is due to the introduction of whiteboards and electronic blackboards. When they heard that the company was closing, mathematicians and teachers, two groups that still use blackboards, raised their voices to appeal for it to stay in business.

Indeed, the process of doing and teaching mathematics is still built around writing continuous lines on blackboards. That is, mathematical dialogue arises from that mysterious relationship between the rate of thinking of the one who writes and the rate of comprehension of the one who reads. Perhaps the type of thinking required to explain formulas is fundamentally incompatible with the act of hitting keyboard keys. I believe the dance-like movements engendered by blackboard and chalk, which enable the user to write out results as fast as they can think them, act in concert with the intellectual rhythms that set mathematical thinking in motion. Most people assume mathematics must necessarily refer to cutting-edge technology. This impression doesn't just surprise mathematicians. It shocks them.

I forget where and when I witnessed it, but I have a memory of watching a mathematician string together endless, winding formulas on a blackboard. When the blackboard was finally covered from corner to corner, the mathematician moved to another blackboard on a different wall and continued writing. Hagoromo chalk, with its smooth, silky performance, its very substance, must have been integral to the link between brain and body the mathematician relied on. Chalk users' reaction to Hagoromo's closing mirrors the current feelings of professional photographers who now have to purchase and stockpile film and printing paper to protect it from being swept away by the wave of digitization. One media outlet reported that a certain mathematics professor at Stanford University bought and stocked fifteen years' worth of chalk. An indication of how chalk users feel about the preservation of a form of thinking and its physical counterpart, which is so integral to their craft.

Incidentally, Hagoromo means "garment of feathers"—a wonderful name. It reminds me of something a heavenly maiden would wear—a white, semi-transparent, and, most of all, soft garment. The patent for the technology that made their chalk so successful was in the end transferred to another company, so it seems that the special innovations that created this chalk will live on. When white is brought up, we often think of paper. Like a moment of clarity arising out of the mists of the early dawn, however, stories like Hagoromo's emerge to remind us that white is also present in the chalk-written characters and formulas that float across blackboards.

042 Wrinkles

At first glance, wrinkles seem like ugly blemishes. Humans, ignorant of the natural conditions of life, judge "tautness" and "wrinkles" to be bitterly at odds with each other. As a result, we do all that we can to restore tension to our spirits and bodies, both of which tend to droop when we let our guard down. We associate the tautness of smooth skin with vitality or youth and wrinkles with worry or old age. Thus, we admire the attempt to get rid of the latter and strive for the former.

A poster framer is someone who brings out the "tautness" in things. The paper used in a work of calligraphy, for example, may become wrinkled from the invasive effects of water and ink. This paper once again becomes wonderfully flat in the hands of a skilled framer. And once such a worker mounts and hangs a scroll, the calligraphy exudes an elegance that reverberates through the viewer's mind and body. Facing such a work, one is compelled to stand up straight and look back in a correspondingly dignified way. I would say that this feeling of renewal and reinvigoration is like the moment when you take in your hands a smartly pressed dress shirt just picked up from the cleaners.

We are not like paper, and we have no choice but to accept wrinkles on our bodies. They are our destiny. Perhaps because they are inevitable I have, oddly enough, come to feel a certain affection for them. "Wrinkled" realism against "taut" idealism—perhaps I sense in that opposition some fundamental law harkening to the transitory nature of all things.

I once ran a one-year seminar on wrinkles with a class of graduating students at the arts college where I teach. The aim was to get the students to question their values, to shed the biases they had unknowingly accumulated. I made wrinkles the class theme. One student conceived a project called "Sent Wrinkles" that centered on the various folds, crushing, and creasing that paper endures in the mailing process as it travels to its destination. The project involved sending to Tokyo packages from various cities around the world. These items included envelopes with thin sponges inside, or items packed in thirty-by-thirty-centimeter-square sheets of white envelopes. As a result, we received truly beautiful wrinkles from all over the world. Or at least, I should say we received packaging that had acquired creases en route to us. It was as if the mailing process was a petri dish for cultivating antiques. The parcels travelled great distances, passed through countless hands, and experienced extremes of heat, cold, and humidity; some of them encountered rain or snow, and all were tossed and buffeted in bins and scraped on conveyor belts, leaving them with a vast number of bumps and bruises.

Packages that originally bore not even the slightest crinkle were thus transformed into soiled, off-white, artistic accumulations of creases. Some packages were rewrapped or lost. Those that found their way back to us were displayed alongside a chart showing their route. The personality these countless packages and envelopes had acquired on their migration through space-time was striking. Just as remarkable was the idea itself—using mail as a generative and representational wrinkle machine. Perhaps I was so moved because I felt as though it was me that had been extracted from a tattered parcel and put up on display this inexorably decaying me that fades a little more each time it collides with the countless obstacles of time and space that are life.

043 Hemp

Hemp cloth has a smooth, stiff feel. One of its defining features is the way its surface develops a lovely collection of wrinkles and creases. We have lived with hemp since antiquity, it is said. What makes us so perpetually fascinated by the material?

Hemp is a plant that grows quickly and matures vigorously; yet it is an annual and thus dies each year. We lay claim to hemp's vitality by spinning its stem fibers into threads and weaving them into cloth, turning it into a gift that we then enjoy. It was once classified as a "textile," its production considered an industry worthy of imperial support. But it can also be simply called "cloth." Perhaps the emperor singled it out because it best captured the fruit of the farmers' labor, or because it embodied the harvesting of nature's blessings. Hemp woven into magnificent patterns strikes people as an exquisite accomplishment. People are inevitably moved, too, by its whiteness, brimming as it is with a radiance that washes over our hearts. Even today, natural, undyed hemp cloth is considered exceptionally beautiful.

However, hemp's attraction is not solely derived from freshly woven cloth, so impressive it seems to glow. I think we also have to acknowledge its beauty when it is shabby and old, threatening to disintegrate back into undifferentiated earth.

We wash clothes, then dry them in sunlight. These crisp, clean clothes carry the scent of the sun. We wear them and sweat in them. The clothes soak up the sweat, so we wash and dry them again. This repetitive process, despite appearances, is never unproductive. For along with this repetition, slowly but surely, comes a fulfilling sense of being alive. Unbleached hemp clothing gets whiter every time it is washed and dried. With each wash the fabric's minute fibers become more frayed, rub against each other, and weaken, until the cloth loses its original shape. Finally, it tears. What was clothing becomes a rag.

Now it has a new job as a dish towel or a duster. Then, it becomes even more worn in its new, harsh, utility-driven environment.

Woven so that when new it practically glows, hemp absorbs bodily fluids, and later can be used to clear grime from our dwelling places. It is rinsed out countless times with water, and then basks and dries again in sunlight. And each time it goes through this process, it gains back some of its whiteness—again and again and again. Has this process not seeped into our own emotional rhythms, becoming a part of our very being? The way hemp ages and disintegrates, its very simplicity, parallels our own life course—it is a guardian of our deepest sensibilities.

In Europe, before the use of wood pulp, scraps of clothing were used to make paper. Twisted, worn-out hemp fibers were perfect for this. Old clothes were thoroughly pulverized, dispersed in water and then, as pulp, spread thin and lifted out to dry. Once dried in the sunlight it once again developed a fresh tautness, and brand-new hemp paper was born.

044 Silk

When I hear the words "Silk Road," I always imagine the broad high-way of commerce that once linked the Western world and East Asia. I sense its incredible vastness. In my twenties I thought I would try traveling the Road. The planned trip, however, coincided exactly with the Soviet Union's invasion of Afghanistan, so I abandoned it. Silk certainly was not the sole good that was traded on the Silk Road, but given its shiny appearance and smooth beauty, and humankind's eternal desire to trade, it is easy to understand and sympathize with the merchants who sought it out and organized caravans to take it to far-off markets. The desire is transhistorical—humankind will always pursue beauty and the unknown.

Silk is thought to have been invented in China. Its production there is shown to have begun in about 3,000 BCE. Even if it had accomplished nothing else, I believe China's greatness would have been recognized for this single achievement—for creating such an elegant fabric from silkworm cocoons. The Chinese of ancient times already possessed an impeccable eye for selecting the highest quality goods and exploring all avenues to improve manufacturing methods. The basis for what is now called sericulture was established in the Han dynasty—that is, just before the beginning of the common era. It was highly developed and included, among other techniques, a system of raising and caring for silkworms in specially designed rooms, and various methods for storing their eggs.

Perhaps because human history is so often seen through the lens of technological development, there is a tendency to assume that the intellectual and emotional capacities of ancient peoples—i.e. those who lacked highly advanced technology—somehow pale in comparison with people today. This is flat-out wrong. Does one form of intelligence outweigh the other? Is the superior intelligence the one that installs machines and robots to maximize productivity and profit? Or is it the one that resolves to seek out the absolute value of things? Ancient people certainly had this latter form of intelligence. The "wisdom" of the people of today, by contrast, devotes itself to processing goods as efficiently as possible with ever more incomprehensible machinery.

Silk thread is made by first twisting together the extremely fine fibers the silkworm produces for its cocoon. Those threads are then woven together. This innovation, the discovery of weaving, was a stroke of pure genius. It meant converting a natural substance into homogeneous "threads," spinning those threads into a material that could be more easily worked with, and then turning that material into cloth. It is painstaking work. But as a reward for the strain inflicted on the body and mind of the weaver, an exquisitely formed object emerges. It is a system still in use today. The process of crafting cloth from thread is itself beautiful, whether done by hand or with a loom. Indeed, through careful technique, a loom can come to feel like an extension of the body. It is as though through weaving we discovered our self-awareness, perfected our sense of time, learned to think and breathe. The more masterful the craftsperson, the more uniform the finished cloth. Silk's alluring luster is pure elegance. We may live in a human-centered world, but in silk we can see clearly embodied both the acquired blessings of nature and an inherently valuable sense of what we have achieved.

Why does the silkworm produce not a blue, red, or black fiber, but a white one? Why a white cocoon? Only the gods can tell. But as a result, a massive trade route was born stretching across Eurasia called the "Silk Road."

045 Cotton

Among all textiles cotton is without a doubt the gentlest on our bodies. While not particularly gorgeous, it is unmatched for simplicity and comfort. It feels neither too restrictive nor too loose, is pleasant against the skin, absorbs sweat, and protects and warms us.

Everything down to its appearance signals softness even when it is unwoven batting. Cotton is a serene, spirit-attracting object like those used in Shinto ceremonies—a *yorishiro*. It embodies and projects a gentle calm that seems almost too good for a world like ours.

"The White Hare of Inaba" is a legend about a hare who deceived sharks by telling them he wanted to count their numbers, but instead used their backs as stepping stones to traverse the ocean. On his way across, the hare was attacked by one of the sharks, who tore off his fur coat. Stripped red and naked, the hare would eventually be found and rescued by Lord Ōkuninushi. But before that, in great pain, he encountered a group of spiteful *kami* who lied to him, telling him that if he washed his body in the ocean and let himself dry, the pain would go away. The hare followed their malicious instructions, but far from being healed, his skin dried out, cracked and split, and his suffering became even worse. Lord Ōkuninushi, who had been tasked with carrying on his back the luggage of the kami, who had gone on ahead, only then came across the hare and took pity on him. He told the hare that he would surely heal if he washed himself in fresh water and then wrapped himself in cattail cotton. Sure enough, after following Lord Ōkuninushi's instructions, the hare recovered. The redness disappeared, and the hare was once again covered in his white fur coat.

Cattail cotton is faintly yellow and feels somewhat coarse. When I hear this story, however, I always imagine pure-white tufts of cotton batting instead. Cotton holds plenty of air, which makes it feel pleasantly fluffy against the skin. Indeed, it is no wonder the hare's coat healed after being washed in fresh water and wrapped in soft downy cotton.

Most quilt batting used today comes from cotton. Raw cotton is sometimes called "cotton flower" in Japanese, but it is in fact a seed pod or boll. A cotton field full of plants bending over with the weight of their pure white, fibrous bolls looks uncannily like a field of snow. The bolls themselves are already fluffy to the touch. Rather than being woven into threads, they can be collected as is and stuffed into quilts and mattresses. Japan's unique form of bedding is the *kake-futon*, a soft cotton-filled quilt that hugs the body. If you are delicate in body or spirit, it will embrace you with a wonderful tenderness and warmth.

In recent years, Western-style beds have become commonplace in Japan. Apparently, fewer people are spreading out mattresses, or *shikibuton*, over tatami. Yet, Japan should take pride in the futon. Unlike most furniture, it is adaptable because it does not have a clear shape or function. That's why we can cuddle up against it in any way our body likes.

Young Japanese children love to make "caves" out of quilts. These kake-futon caves are dark and roomy. Burrow a hole and you can see the bright "outside world" through the gap.

A futon that has been aired in the sunshine smells like the sunny outdoors. Flop down on a sun-dried futon and bury your face in it. All your tension will slowly unravel. Before you know it, the cottony softness may even move you to tears. But be careful—you might have been turned into a white hare!

046 Rice

The Japanese did not cultivate rice. Rather, the people we call "the Japanese" were cultivated by the thing we call rice.

There are many types of grains in the world. Over a long period of time, the West chose wheat, the East rice. The Japanese chose a specific type of rice at that, the short-grained variety that becomes glossy and sticky when cooked. Lift a steaming clump of rice to your mouth. Your mouth will fill with a moisture-laden, flavorful chewiness. The more you chew, the more you notice a faint sweetness. Japanese came to believe that seven *kami* dwell within a single grain of rice. I am unsure why the Chinese, so dedicated to refinement, opted for the dryer, long-grained rice. Perhaps they felt it was more compatible with their style of cooking.

Rice is a remarkably productive plant. A single grain, planted in the right conditions, can yield over a thousand grains, all from just that one plant. An annual thousand-fold yield—or more. Before the advent of farming, very few plants growing near one's home could be eaten. Yet at some point, it dawned on our ancestors that they could sow the seeds of edible grains about their dwelling place. After an incredible amount of trial and error, they found one specifically suited to the climate and soil of their region. Finally, at the end of a dizzyingly long span of time, rice filtered into Japan's natural topography, where it slowly took root.

There are a number of theories about when exactly Japanese history began. If you start with the late Jomon period, when rice cultivation had already begun, it goes back more than 2,500 years. Since that time, each and every year, people have prayed to the gods of heaven and earth for the success of the rice crop. Sometimes these prayers were met with the relief of an abundant harvest; at other times the crop was poor. In either case, Japanese lived on rice and alongside rice. Their hearts and minds became attuned to the growth of rice. The passing of a year was synonymous with the rice life-cycle. That way of life endured until very recently, changing only after the Second World War, when Japan became an industrialized country.

Terraced rice paddies were cultivated across the river-rich, mountainous regions, crisscrossing the land like the contour lines on a topographical map. These terraces were like dams, protecting the slopes from flooding and landslides. The leftovers of rice harvesting were turned into straw, which then was made into ropes and bags. These were used as vessels for storing rice or eggs, as raincoats to ward off rain and snow, as sandals to protect the feet, or as the softer straw of tatami. They were even used as the raw material for *shimekazari* —festoons of straw ropes—and other ritual items in the offering of prayers and blessings.

Sake was also distilled from rice. To the Japanese one of the most important aspects of food is whether it is in season, i.e. whether it is in harmony with the rich diversity of the four seasons. We do not merely enjoy the flavor of fish, for example, but also delight in its freshness. The subtle, sweet taste of sake complements this freshness. The bran that remains after rice is milled is salted and used to aid food fermentation. The lees left over from sake-making are also used in specific types of food. Nothing is wasted. Everything has its use.

Traveling in Japan, you can see rice fields in the distance from your train window. During rice-planting season they are glittering pools of water reflecting the sky. In summer, they are lush and green, instilling a feeling of hope. In the fall, the wind sends wave-like ripples through an ocean of heavy, bowing rice heads. And within each golden husk is a grain housing seven kami.

047 Mochi

Freshly cooked rice is of course a staple of our diet, but *mochi* is also a highly significant part of Japanese food culture. The fact that there are both round and square versions of mochi seems somehow typically human. We like round things, but we like square things just as much. Freshly pounded mochi is rolled in small spheres by hand and made into *dango*—sweet mochi dumplings. It is also flattened to make rounded *maru-mochi*. The rectangular *kaku-mochi* is made by stretching out mochi until it has a smooth surface and then cutting it at right angles. Either boiled or grilled, all these will take on a characteristically soft, stretchy stickiness. Try to bite off a piece and the mochi will stretch from your mouth in a long string. But this is nothing like the tough, unmanageable elasticity of rubber. Rather, it is resistant, but just tender enough to bite through. And once you begin eating, you will find it perfectly chewy. It fills the inside of your mouth with the special pleasure of biting, chewing, and swallowing something that is somehow exactly the right texture and consistency.

When I eat a marbled, perfectly grilled piece of wagyu beef, I sometimes feel a certain drunkenness at that moment the fatty red meat gently melts on my tongue. That same euphoria grips me when I eat mochi. This is not food that one can savor every day. Experiencing it daily would cheapen this extreme sense of satisfaction. Perhaps this is why Japanese people only eat mochi on special occasions, like New Year's Day. We are normally content with our daily routine, cooking regular rice or some other grain. But on special days we use mochi rice—sometimes to make *sekihan* or *okowa* and sometimes pounded to make *mochitsuki*. If regular rice signifies luck, then mochi signifies great fortune, and is connected to very auspicious occasions.

Of course, the institution of rice as the basis of the Japanese diet was not decreed by some great, wise leader. The custom formed organically, out of the ordinary practical wisdom of people who over a long period of time incorporated the grain into their everyday eating habits. That is how it reached its value and place in society. While it is crucial, in Japanese culture, to resist the temptations of luxury, it is just as important to dedicate ourselves to preserving objects of excellence over the long run. In other words, to integrate them into our daily lives. I believe that mochi is an example of this.

Mochi stuffed with *anko*—sweet red bean paste—is called *daifuku-mochi*, literally "great luck" mochi. Smear the circumference of a mochi ball with anko or soybean flour and you will have *o-hagi*, also called *botamochi*. Mochi by itself is filled with the thrill of celebration. Add a little sweetness to it, though, and you get a food bursting with festivity. "Great luck"—a fitting name indeed. Almost a type of *o-hagi*, daifuku would never be mistaken for a staple food, fitting better in the category of "sweets." Still, it behaves almost like a side dish with its stubbornly modest flavor, resonating with the likes of *shiokara* and *umeboshi*, miso and soy sauce, spicy mustard and wasabi. And yet, it feels like a "sweet" when, unlike cooked rice—the reigning monarch of staple foods—it unleashes a whole set of wonderful sensations that are not experienced every day. Ah, the wonders of mochi....

There is also a New Year's decoration called *kagami-mochi* —mirror-shaped mochi. It is made of two rounded, slightly flattened mochi balls, a small one placed atop another, over which you set a mandarin or bitter orange. This shape reflects the spirit of a prayer for the smooth unfolding of the coming year. The two joined parts of kagami-mochi embody and celebrate the great fortune of an auspicious occasion.

048 Udon

Udon's most attractive features are its springy elasticity and firm texture. This is a food to be masticated by the masses, whose strong molars can bite down on anything—no matter how hard—without risk of breaking. It was not made for the teeth of elites overly accustomed to eating soft things. This is what makes it so delicious.

Sanuki udon has that bite; it stimulates our instinct to eat and then calms even the most wildly ferocious of appetites. Such is the unique sense we get from this food, which comes from the island of Shikoku. *Sanuki udon* is made to be eaten simply and honestly. It possesses the spirit of the traditional foods of this region. This is especially true of the *kamatama*, "broth-splashed" varieties.

The broth of these dishes has an *iriko*—dried sardine—base. To this base is added a relatively rich soy sauce along with citrus fruit native to Shikoku. *Yuzu* or a fruit-juice vinegar can also be added. To make the udon noodles, you thoroughly knead wheat-flour dough and cut it lengthwise. Even today, udon makers refrain from using machines, opting instead to step on a piece of plastic over the dough, because that is what produces the udon's characteristic gummy, firm texture. Not even *mochi* or *dango* can compete with the elasticity of udon noodles that have been steamed and cooked inside a kama pot. Ladle the wriggling noodles into a *donburi* bowl as the steam rises around you. Without pausing, crack an egg and drop it in. Add a small amount of the strong broth. Arranging some sliced spring onions or pickled ginger over the top, lightly swish the noodles with chopsticks from side to side, and then slurp some up. You will feel no urge to speak to others around you until the bowl is finished. This food-induced silence is due to your instinctive desire to devour that paradise sitting right before your eyes.

In Japanese, the mimetic word *shikoshiko* fits perfectly here. It describes something that looks soft but is unexpectedly firm. Something that resists when you bite down on it but that you can nonetheless cut with your teeth. Something that responds to your desire to chew it. The udon itself, like cooked rice and mochi, has a delicate flavor. Mix yellow egg yolk into steaming white noodles and add a small amount of broth. A happy feeling of harmony will rise from your mouth all the way to your nose.

Daylight lasts much longer in Shikoku's Kagawa Prefecture, which is perfect for growing grain crops. The reason udon is made from wheat flour is that both rice and wheat are harvested twice a year. Yet the prefecture receives little rainfall and has few rivers, so sources of water for agriculture can be unreliable. Even today, water reservoirs dot the landscape. Storing flour thus naturally developed from the need to stock grains for longer periods. Originally, white flour was used as insurance against famine, to have at the ready in the case of a poor rice harvest.

Mill wheat into flour, knead it well, and you have a pure white, elastic dough. Such modest colors are certainly not in vogue these days. Yet udon remains plump and white. What is more, the sanuki udon that swept across Japan now circles the globe.

049 Sōmen

Sōmen is a thin, round noodle made with a unique stretching method. The process differs across Japan, depending on the region, but the general idea is to make a wheat-flour dough and then knead and stretch it into the longest strands possible. Nowadays machines do the stretching, but the work was once done by hand, alternating between pulling and then folding the dough over on itself. Once the desired thinness is attained, the noodles are slung over a pair of round poles in a figure eight while being twisted. They are then stretched and allowed to set. The process is repeated. Finally, the noodles are hung vertically and allowed to dry. Once dry, they are cut to the same length and arranged in bundles. A U-shaped portion remains on the poles, called *fushimen*, which is cut up into random lengths and used for a variety of cooking purposes.

In fact, you can shape kneaded flour dough any way you want. Look at, say, Italian pastas. Cylindrical shapes with a spiraling structure, shapes that resemble bow ties, shells, or ribbons—there is truly an enormous variety. Such diversity is also possible with Japan's wheat-flour doughs. But to turn this dough into a string-like noodle —that was a stroke of genius. *Sōmen*, of course, like all wheat-flour noodles, has little inherent flavor. It requires a sauce or *tsuyu* to be truly enjoyed. It can clump while being boiled causing the mass's center to be left undercooked. A uniform thickness ensures that the tsuyu has enough surface area to adhere to. The stretching method seeks to control for all of these factors. This is the perennial challenge for cooks molding foods out of flour.

Perhaps the Italians, belonging to the culture that produced Michelangelo and sharing his desire to shape and sculpt, were not satisfied with string-shaped pasta, and thus developed three-dimensional macaroni. And perhaps the Japanese aesthetic preference for plain over fancy led us to develop simple string-like noodles, in many shapes and thicknesses. The shape of Italian macaroni might not seem overly complex but look closely and you will see it is a well-plotted design. The deeply set creases on the pasta's surface allow sauce to collect there. But let me return to sōmen.

Essentially, sōmen is the thinnest of udon-type noodles. They are thin but round, not flat, which is crucial. The noodles nestle together in skeins or loops much more easily than if they were square-shaped. Tsuyu naturally collects in these round nests while you slurp the noodles up. Eat them cold and you will feel refreshingly cool. When Japanese elected to form wheat into string-like shapes, the question of whether to cut the finished dough with a knife to form flat noodles or to stretch it out to form round ones was decided only after carefully considering which option was more compatible with tsuyu.

As a summer food, the round, cool sōmen is easy on the palate. Scoop up the noodles from your *donburi* bowl or ice-filled water bucket. Dip them in your tsuyu and quickly suck them up in one satisfying, noisy slurp.

050 Tofu

Tofu is eaten with chopsticks. I suppose the reason Westerners do not eat cold tofu is because chopsticks are not customary. Eating tofu with a knife and fork feels somehow disappointing, as though implements and food are mismatched. Indeed, Western cutlery must have developed together with the practice of meat-eating. It was necessary to have implements that could exert enough force to cut through thick pieces of meat. Forks and knives are ill suited to soft, light food like tofu. Some say spoons can be surprisingly useful here. I have seriously considered this claim, but still feel no attraction to spoons.

Chopsticks are capable of a diverse set of actions—plucking, pinning, raking, pinching, scooping, mixing. They are like long, tapering prosthetic fingers. Further, they are sensory extensions of our real fingers—in other words, their tips are like antennae. Japanese people are always mindful of how they move these acutely sensitive antennae to avoid disturbing the arrangement of the food. Chopsticks are built for precise and efficient eating without extraneous movement. We are well aware of this even as we place food in our mouths.

There are many kinds of tofu, but the most basic form is probably chilled tofu—*hiyayakko*. This white square is most beautiful when placed on a dark flat plate, one with pronounced corners. Sprinkle on dried *bonito* flakes and top it off with finely cut green onions or ginger. Drizzle on a generous amount of soy sauce. Slice off an appropriately sized portion with your chopsticks. Then, gently squeeze that piece and deliver it to your mouth. Tofu is so delicate that pinching it too hard will break it. It becomes difficult to manage once broken apart. So, wield your chopsticks with a careful yet confident touch. Next, take up more than just the tofu. Arrange a small quantity of the bonito flakes, grated ginger, or minced green onion sitting on top, determining the perfect ratio in relation to the size of the tofu piece you have cut. Then pick up the tofu and seasoning and carry them into your mouth. The chopsticks play a crucial role in finishing off the dish in that they allow you to balance the amounts of tofu and condiment.

Boiled tofu is also delicious. *Konbu* is simmered in an off-white, earthenware pot with identically-sized pieces of tofu. Done. People will joke that, "I'm especially good at making boiled tofu." Indeed, the dish is the definition of simplicity. However, eating it is another matter. You must use the chopsticks decisively so that the tofu does not slip. Breaking the tofu within the *nabe* pot is unacceptable, even unrefined. Never pierce the tofu with the tips of your chopsticks. There is a tool called a "tofu scoop," a cleverly crafted implement with a finely woven copper wire mesh. In a single, swift motion, scoop up the tofu from the boiling pot. Transfer it to your small, individual bowl filled with a condiment of your choice, or *tsuyu*. Neatly carve off a single bite with your chopsticks. Lift this white mass, enveloped in steam, to your mouth.

051 Onigiri

I always feel happy when I'm making *onigiri*. Holding warm rice seems to give me a direct line to plenitude and well-being. Whether I plan on eating it myself or am making one for someone else, it is pleasurable to watch rice steadily take shape until it forms a neat parcel that snugly fits in my hands. What a satisfying thing to do.

Freshly cooked rice is hot. You cannot easily mold it at this temperature. So, first cool the rice by lightly spreading it out in a round, wooden *ohitsu*. A hinoki cypress ohitsu is best since it absorbs some of the extra moisture. The cooked rice grains will stick to your fingers and palms if your hands are dry, so lightly moisten them with water. Now, take a small pinch of salt with the fingers of your right hand, and sprinkle it on the palm of your left. Scoop up some rice from the ohitsu with a rice ladle and place it on the salted palm. Place your chosen ingredient in the center and mold the onigiri around it. I seem to be better at triangular onigiri. I was not taught to do it this way, but whatever my intention, the onigiri naturally forms a triangle. Squeeze the rice softly, rotate it, and squeeze again. Repeat this and you will inevitably end up with an onigiri.

As for the ingredients, *umeboshi* (sour plum), walleye pollock roe, and salted salmon are standard. Sometimes salted salmon roe or sea urchin is used. For some reason, the most common are red, warm-colored ingredients. I am not sure who invented umeboshi, but it is clearly at the top of list. The Japanese flag comes to mind.

In my home, whenever we go cherry blossom viewing we always pack onigiri, usually with salted salmon roe. There is no particular reason for this, though. I once unexpectedly received some high-quality salmon roe from the mother of a friend of my son's when he was in kindergarten. I used it for our cherry viewing onigiri and because it was so delicious, that became our custom. From then on, my family and I have always taken salmon roe onigiri to accompany our cherry viewing. Roe is unwieldy and easily falls apart, so we wrap the onigiri entirely in nori seaweed. The result is jet-black onigiri that are soft and moist. We enjoy these every year underneath cherry trees in full bloom.

Our era of family outings has passed. My son, an only child, has long since become independent. Still, when my wife and I go cherry viewing, we make salmon roe onigiri. Habits are strange things. I have been told to reduce my sugar intake and avoid carbohydrates completely, so I have to refrain from eating my most favorite dishes. But cherry viewing only happens once a year. So, on this day only, I decide to take—or grasp, as one would an onigiri—the initiative and eat the way I like.

Onigiri are especially delicious when cooled to the temperature of their surroundings. But they are not to be put in the refrigerator. *Shio-musubi*, plain salted onigiri, are also delicious—they have neither nori nor an inner ingredient. When a number of them are lined they make a dazzling sight. They are like little buds of happiness set up in a tidy row—just waiting for the right moment to bloom.

052 Arrowroot Noodles

Perhaps semi-transparent, slippery arrowroot noodles so captivate me because, as a living creature myself, I share a similar kind of existence. Not everything about me is clear and distinct. Thinking, breathing, drinking water—these are ambiguous acts. Exactly when do we switch over from the act of "breathing" to the act of "drinking?" We live our lives without being aware of such things. In other words, what we call being alive is an indistinct and slippery condition.

We go about our day-to-day business by sectioning off this ambiguity into work time, sleep time, jog time, commute time, eat time, leisure time, contemplation time, etc. Compartmentalized like a *makunouchi*—literally, "between act"—bento box, our days unfold step by step. This is how we give them meaning. It is a means for us focus our attention. Even at school, the subjects we learn are partitioned—Japanese, arithmetic, science, social studies, the arts, physical education. In other words, a timetable—in Japanese, a "time-split." To "split apart time," we even organize the way we think in the name of efficiency. By adopting such customs, we may unintentionally create an overly rigid timetable for our lives.

In truth, however, we instinctively understand the impossibility of making such sharp distinctions. Existence and time, awareness and life: these concepts sometimes run together, but sometimes flow apart. Everything fluctuates, in concert with the rhythms of the universe. Somehow, things appear out of chaos. Slowly their shapes are revealed. But just when they are on the cusp of becoming bold and distinct, they may grow blurred and hazy, slowly returning to the amorphous chaos. Our conceptions of the world, our thinking, our bodies, our very lives take part in this cycle. We do not strike out to reach a clear-cut destination, based on intention. Rather, like jellyfish, we float about in the space-time of the universe. As a result, looking at arrowroot noodles feels like confronting the uncertainty of our existence. Perhaps this is why our hearts beat faster.

Arrowroot noodles, or *kuzukiri*, are made from the starchy flour of ground arrowroot, or *kuzu*, roots: they are the solidified result of mixing arrowroot flour with water. They have little flavor, as one would expect from their semi-transparent appearance. Nor do they have the firmness of white rice. Frankly, kuzukiri is eaten only very occasionally as a snack between meals, or perhaps offered after meals in a dessert dish. For me, it is peaceful at first to watch the slithery, insubstantial noodles settling into the bottom of a black lacquer bowl. Gradually, though, it comes to feel as if my own nebulous essence has been starkly laid out before me. The whitish arrowroot noodles are barely visible against the universe-harkening black lacquer bowl. I gently drizzle brown sugar syrup over them. Then I randomly pinch them with my chopsticks and lift them to my mouth. They lack the bite of agar jelly. Instead, a rich, honey-like sweetness saturates my mouth. With the sense of uncertainty still lingering, I gulp the noodles down.

There is an old word referring to that point in the evening when it becomes difficult to discern the face of someone approaching you: *tasokare*—literally, "who is that?" Essentially, the word means "dusk." The barely-there whiteness of arrowroot noodles quietly recalls that brief, uncertain moment.

053 Mist and Light

Hasegawa Tōhaku's *Pine Tree* Screens is a set of ink wash paintings from the Momoyama period. One can intuitively see its resemblance to Claude Monet's *Water Lilies* series, the impressionist masterpiece of the early twentieth century.

The best place to see Monet's *Water Lilies* is the Musée de l'Orangerie in Paris. The space is designed to accommodate a group of paintings in the series, which are arranged along a gently curving wall so that natural light falls on them at a changing angle, bringing the lilies into relief, ever so softly. For some reason, tears come to my eyes whenever I view these paintings. I am moved not just by their beauty, but by the realization that painting can achieve such heights.

Monet depicts not only a pond dense with water lilies, but also the sky and the various qualities of light diffused through the ambient air and reflected on the pond's surface. Monet endlessly confronts the stubborn reality that our world is revealed to us by light. In so doing he encounters a fundamental law of the universal. What amazing eyes he must have had—eyes that saw into the universal foundations of life. The lilies were nothing more than an excuse, an opportunity. He was really depicting light.

And what of the *Pine Trees Screens?* The pine trees are painted in ink with rough brush strokes. Yet one gets the impression that it is the open, unpainted portions that have the most vitality, and that this is the underlying motif of this and other ink paintings. The areas of opaque white are empty, yet they have atmospheric weight, like a mist or haze. The unpainted space does not depict nothingness or the mere absence of the pine trees; it is a terrifying blankness—in Japanese, an "empty whiteness"—that our imagination strives to fill. Perhaps just beyond this barrier of cloud there are ranks of pine tree groves, one after another, stretching into the distance.... Or perhaps what is concealed behind the curtain of mist is an unimaginable spectacle. The painting also depicts a white mountain in the distance, what must be a sacred mountain. Indeed, it is no exaggeration to say that most of the landscape, from pine forest to mountain, is invisible, hidden from us, creating a feeling of breathless suspense.

The rough brushwork used to depict the pines moors us to their reality while our eyes and heart float away into the misty, blank space. The very life of the painting resides in this sensation. The blank spaces and margins—the "remaining whiteness"—allow our imagination to spread its wings freely. The Japanese arts are designed to act in concert with such spaces. The *Pine Trees Screens* is the epitome of that style.

The aim of this painting is not representation. Rather, it is a means through which one can speculate about the world. Common to impressionism and Japanese painting—an absolute, perhaps, that both seek to attain—is the desire to convey a perpetually moving vagueness, a play of mist and light. Whether they reach that absolute is not the point. They open the floodgates of the viewer's imagination, allowing it to gush forth. Moreover, that imagination is absorbed into the painting, which becomes a vessel that carries the vision across time.

054 Sakura

Drop a single pickled *sakura*—cherry blossom—petal into a *hakuji* tea bowl filled with plain hot water. The water will turn a faint pink and release a scent reminiscent of the sakura flower itself.

The weeping cherry trees of Kyoto are beautiful. Indeed, they are magical. And yet, I have come to believe that the sakura that inhabits the hearts of the Japanese is neither the *somei-yoshino* cherry, the weeping cherry, nor the mountain cherry. Rather, it is the ideal image of sakura.

When we say "the Imperial Palace," we mean the area beyond the moat. To the people walking the Tokyo streets, it is an inaccessible wilderness. Citygoers gaze at its transcendent nature from our concrete-bound side of the bank, and see it as the quintessence of a calm, even remote, originary topography. The French critic Roland Barthes once proclaimed that "emptiness" occupies the heart of Japan. Indeed, the Japanese style refrains from placing anything at the center, choosing to leave it empty. We refrain from definitions and assertions of significance. It is through this empty middle ground that we convey everything—with a silence-preserving nod. Japanese have come to a mutual understanding through the sign called nothingness. Even today, the huge metropolis of Tokyo has at its precise center the emptiness that is the Imperial Palace. That fundamental aspect of Japan has not changed. The very fact that the palace is a symbol establishes it as a blank canvas with unlimited potential meanings. By avoiding definitions, we leave room for infinite interpretations.

Sakura season comes to the Imperial Palace each year. The gentle scent, hue, swelling, blooming, and falling has a timeless elegance that stirs up something deep inside us. The tree bears so many wondrous flowers. The Japanese sensibility of *mono no aware*—the sad but beautiful transience of all things—epitomizes the expressive quality unique to sakura: the first signs that the flowers will begin to bloom, the charm of the blossoms as they gently open, the chaos of full bloom, and the sense of impermanence as the blooms begin to fall. Like a flowing river, nothing about sakura stays still—as the trees convey sorrow, at times pain, at times fortune, and at times glory. Things will soon change, nothing lasts forever—this sentiment is at the heart of the spirit of Japan. As I have written, Japanese culture revolves around fragility, caution, subtlety, and brevity. But these words reference only the outward appearance of things. The way you internalize these perspectives is by understanding that all is transient—by accepting, in other words, what is summarized as "impermanence" or *mujoukan*, an important Buddhist concept.

I once went to visit the sakura trees lining the Chidoriga-fuchi moat at the Imperial Palace in the middle of the night. They were in full bloom—I could feel their profusion masked in darkness on the other side of the moat. Their intensity, encompassing both madness and sanity. An enormous mass of whiteness possessing limitless energy. Through all of this, I felt the country called Japan.

Let me die in spring beneath the blossoming trees,
Under the full moon of Kisaragi.

The Yoshino sakura once loved by the poet Saigyō and the sakura of Chidoriga-fuchi may look slightly different, but to die beneath any sakura requires a unique form of determination and resignation. By no means would it be a peaceful death.

055 Wax

In Ehime Prefecture, lying between the cities of Matsuyama and Uwajima, is a town called Uchiko that has carefully preserved its traditional streets. One attractive feature of Japan's old villages is the tiled roofs that line the streetscape. Their low, thick eaves and the shadows they cast are an essential part of the visual effect. The roads are interwoven shadow and light, chains of dark patterns. Because entranceways, fences, and windows—parts of any functional architecture—face the street, the various depths and intensities of shadow produce a distinctive rhythm. From this rhythm emerges a townscape based on gradation. Wooden grates and doors, white plaster and *namako* walls, blackened from the passing of an era, accent this gradation in a pleasing way.

Uchiko once flourished as a manufacturing hub for Japan wax, a special compound used for candles. The old wax-production houses preserved in the center of town hint at this past prosperity. You can still see in these Japanese-style houses remnants of the candle-production equipment, tucked away in corners and gardens. Looking about the houses, which sprawl across magnificent plots of land, you can sense what it must have been like to live here in the old days. The age before electric light illuminated the night.... Not so long ago. Life is more convenient with electric lights, we're told, but is this true? I expect those who lived when bonfires or candles were the only illumination were more sensitive to the partnership of darkness and light. Sadly, we moderns no longer pay any attention to the darkness; we swept it away, turning night into high noon. What stands out most in Tokyo's nightscape are the pale lights of convenience stores and vending machines. No longer are these lights considered beautiful, however. Now they strike us as painfully empty. We approach death with a machine that takes over our breathing, our bodies skewered with countless, life-prolonging tubes. There is something unbearable about this.

Japanese candles were first made when the envoy to Tang dynasty China brought back beeswax. Bonfires have been a custom since ancient times, and the practice of lighting them with a wick dipped in oil has existed for almost as long. The "wax" was removed from plants and animals and rolled into a cylinder with a fibrous wick at its center, to form a lamp. This provided steady light until the wax burned away. What an epochal idea.

The sixteenth century—the beginning of Japan wax production. Crush and then steam the outer layer of a lacquer tree, also called wax tree fruit. Compress the result, squeezing out the main ingredient for the wax. Expose this to sunlight. What results is white wax.

Japanese candles gently fan out near the top. This characteristic shape enables the quiet, humble act of what we call "presenting a sacred light to the darkness." It is a shape that resonates deep within our hearts. Countless white candles lined up in the dark.... Imagining this I feel the darkness start to tremble, as if it were breathing, alive.

056 Limestone Caves

Limestone caves are a natural phenomenon. In fact, there is one such cave, Ikura-do, in my home prefecture, Okayama. I recall visiting it with my family when I was a small child, before entering elementary school. The mysteries of the natural processes that shaped the inner cave had a big impact on my youthful mind. The strange forms I saw there are imprinted somewhere deep within my memory.

Limestone dissolved by flowing water over very long stretches of time produces large cavities. Add still more years and strange-looking white masses form, the result of calcium-enriched water dripping from the ceiling. The astonishing time scale involved is what makes them so impressive. The icicle-like shapes formed from the drips are called stalactites, while the masses that rise from the floor like bamboo shoots are stalagmites. When these two phenomena finally enter into contact and merge, you have stone pillars. Apparently, stalactites and stalagmites take over a millennium to form—depending on a variety of factors, it could take decades or even centuries for them to grow a single centimeter.

These shapes are the result of a single calcium-rich drip, an unflagging tip-tap crystallizing over a span that dwarfs the scale of a human life. Moreover, these calcifications—both dissolving into water and reforming via the flow of water—derive from deposits that originated from the bones of coral and other sea creatures. The remains of those unimaginably ancient life forms were lifted up from the bottom of the ocean and moved to the surface by changes in the earth's crust. The thought is mind-boggling. Inevitably, I am made to think about how very fleeting my time here on the surface of the earth is.

We hold this reality unconsciously. What is more, I believe we tacitly consent to it. Something resembling a limestone cave exists within all of us. Take, for example, the fact that we have two eyes symmetrically arranged, and that our arms and legs are also bilateral. Now, I have little reason to complain that I had no say in how my body is formed. Its shape was determined in advance of my inhabiting it. But surely there were other possibilities. Nonetheless, my eyes and legs are symmetrical. Human symmetry is like a leaf's; we are a coordinated whole split in half from head to feet. Intersecting that line is yet another line of symmetry, a horizontal one. These two lines are at right angles. I believe this is a matter of some significance. In the process of living in and mastering this right-angled body of ours, we have naturally come to arrange our personal environments in sets of squares. In other words, square living spaces are the result of the endless movements of our body. We build walls, doors, windows, and desks in that manner. Square cities arise from the accumulation of all these squares. Our environment has taken form through this invisible cause-and-effect relationship. Perhaps our skyscrapers and partitioned land unknowingly reflect natural formations like those in limestone caves. We call the things we make artificial. Yet in view of the ceaseless passage of time, this "artificiality" may be entirely within nature's domain.

057 Clouds

I understand that white clouds are collections of water and ice particles. Yet I find it somehow difficult to experience them that way. The forms clouds take are just too wonderful and mysterious. Looking down on a sea of clouds from an airplane is for me the best way to view them. However, perhaps because I have become so used to the flying experience, I no longer feel quite as impressed by this as I once did. It's amazing how even extraordinary things can become ordinary—like being borne along at high altitude in a flying ship with solid wings and fuselage moving through liquid-like air. Should I find myself in a stricken plane about to crash, I might simply accept it as my fate, because that too has been normalized to some extent. There are places that experience numerous earthquakes and volcanic eruptions. There is also the possibility, however slight, that an enormous meteorite will crash into us. And so, we refuse to worry about things we cannot predict. We board aircraft as if they were utterly ordinary and fly over seas of clouds.

Nevertheless, why are clouds the white they are? Why do they remain so mysterious to us no matter how often we see them? It is said that air is transparent because we have no need to perceive it otherwise. That might indeed be the case. But then, why can we see clouds?

Perhaps creatures that evolved to live on the earth's surface learned things from looking at the clouds. Imagine an ancient time before the dawn of humanity. Changes in the weather must have had a profound influence on the survival of frail, prehistoric creatures. Fluctuations in the flow and shape of clouds portended shifts in the weather. Those creatures must have inferred a great deal from these various signs—whether to prepare for drought or monsoon, for the heat or for the cold. We humans, too, sought to survive by analyzing clouds.

Today, humanity has reached great heights of technological development. We rely on the precise forecasting of weather satellites that tirelessly observe changes in weather. As a result, we no longer direct our senses towards the sky. We no longer read the clouds. Thus, we no longer sense the significance in the shifting white shapes. Yet our senses still retain the ability to see them. That explains why, even today, when we gaze down at an oceanic expanse of clouds from an altitude tens of thousands of meters higher up, we still want to interpret them somehow.

It is common to look down on clouds below from mountains and high plateaus. Gaze up and you will see the air has thinned and the blue sky darkened. You are seeing the blackness of outer space showing through the upper atmosphere. Water circulates in the thin layer of atmosphere that clings to the earth's surface. This water, coaxed by gravity, falls to the earth as rain and flows down mountains and into valleys. Sometimes it seeps underground to create limestone caves and onsen. Sometimes it forms earth-scraping glaciers. Mostly it turns into rivers that head for the ocean, or water vapor that returns to the sky. The clouds that we could read in ages past are illegible now. But, look! There they are.

058 Crystals

When people say "the crystallization of one's effort"—as in the fruits of one's labor—what exact image comes to mind? What kind of crystal do they picture?

Quartz, that is, rock crystal—in Japanese, "water crystal" —first interested me as a boy. The rascal boys in my neighborhood competed to find quartz crystals to see who could impress the others most. These were the common sort of quartz that even we could get our hands on, so they were hardly of impressive size. I recall they were so tiny you might miss them even if they were held in someone's palm. Still, with their hexagonal pillars surrounded by elaborate crystallizations, they were unlike all other stones. These intense, beautiful shapes were right there for the taking. They meshed with our innocent curiosity. Indeed, I was entranced by the crystals. Some supernatural magic principle seemed to be at work in them. We were thrilled that such things were part of the world's mysteries. I searched for them in a quarry where others had apparently found them, but I came out empty-handed.

The first time I saw a "snow crystal" was some time after these boyhood experiences. It was a photo of a snowflake seen through a microscope. I instinctively understood that the same principles that produced the quartz were also at work in the snow crystals, but I was perplexed by how they could make something so delicate and beautiful. I was amazed by the radiance and the perfection of its form. I sat there gazing in fascination.

One need not look beyond earth to experience the abyss that is the universe. Of course, you can get a sense of the endlessness of space by contemplating the Milky Way. But I think examining a crystal rivals this. One finds in it a state of order caused by atoms and molecules that are perfectly balanced. Crystals are fragments that express the providence of the universe through their form. Thinking again about the way those same universal principles are at work in each breath I take gives me the same feeling I have when pondering the endless expanse of ten thousand light years.

I sometimes think that humanity's weakness is found in our sense of "self"—what we call "I." It is a concept manufactured to conveniently rationalize thoughts and actions, forcibly separating into parts the unbreaking flow that is life. I find relief in accepting that "life" does not revolve around me as an individual, but rather that I am a part of the pulse of the universe. Life is just another crystallization. "Death" does not form a binary with life. Rather, it is the counterpart to this "I": my small "self" may die, but life will continue.

Some minerals form perfect cubes. Squares are rarely seen in the natural world since they are unstable compared to hexagons or triangles. Thus, mathematical iterations of four come about only rarely. Yet splendid cubic crystals with a metallic sheen do exist. That they strike me as "artificial" is yet another example of our human delusion.

059 Cutting

Snow falls beautifully onto mud—itself becoming mud.

This is a *haiku* by Ogawa Keishū. The reader is made to feel the beauty of snow's whiteness as it settles on mud. In the next moment, it melts into the mud without a trace.

One of the defining features of haiku poetry is "cutting." A haiku focuses our attention on a single thing so that we are deeply impressed by the atmosphere of that image. Then, punctuating words like "ya" or "kana" are added, to momentarily halt—or cut—the flow of words. These are called "kireji"—"cutting words."

The poet Takahashi Matsuo and I once discussed the notion of "blank space," which he connected to "cutting." He said he felt it expressed the essence of the Japanese sensibility. We see an image and fleetingly become inspired by something we perceive there. When we read a haiku, we imagine the object and then savor the elegance of its depiction in a moment of silence. If we turn back to consider the poem's implications more deeply, we find that there is already nothing there. This sensation is "cutting."

The writer Orikuchi Shinobu likens this to "catching snow." When you catch a snowflake, the sensation lingers in your palm. Yet when you open your hand to look, nothing is there, though you can still feel the cold. Our deepest emotions flow like water—just a moment after we feel them, they are gone without a trace. This is the essential nature of "expression." Of course! I had long felt Japanese were especially able to manage blank space and emptiness to manipulate images. But to think that principle was already at work in "cutting!" It made sense once it was explained to me.

We must not become overly attached to that which moves us. Deep feelings should not be stockpiled like harvested crops.

Impressions engraved on our emotions are like fresh patterns on a pure heart. If we try to keep them, they become ingrained and turn into indelible habits of thinking. Thus, deep passion should last but a moment and then be cut loose. We should always gear our inner selves, our sensibilities, towards brand-new situations. In this approach we can find the mysteries of Japanese expression.

The feeling of being cleansed or purified may also be connected to "cutting." The highest form of expression is nothingness, but this does not refer to a nihility in which nothing can occur. Rather, it is an endless, spacious nothingness: something is captured and shared, then an instant later is dissolved into the senses and purified. This frees your imagination, while at the same time managing whatever visions occur in this freedom until they return to a state of emptiness. Underneath all of this flows a sense of absolute abundance.

White is not the absence of color; it is the saturation of color. The "cutting" aesthetic aims to soften brightly colored after-images and return them to white.

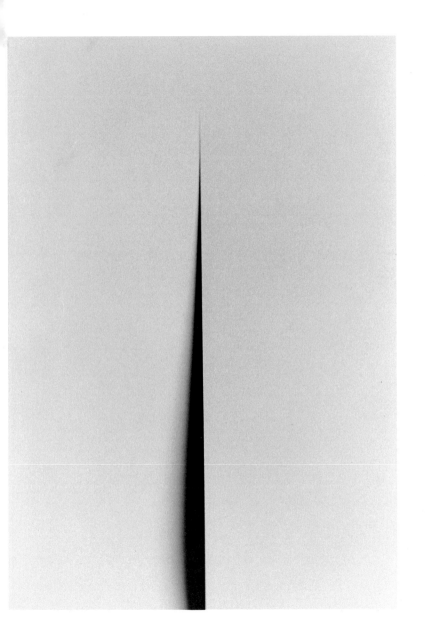

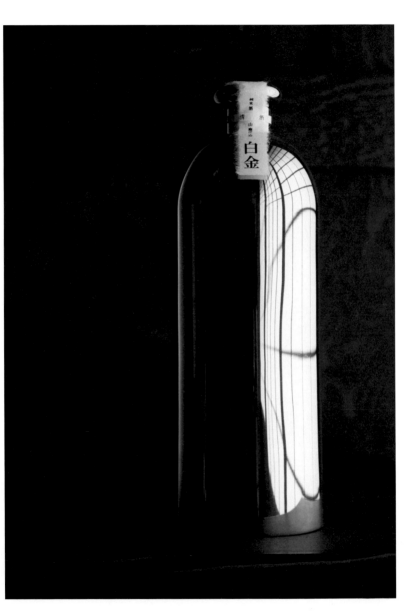

First Page, "Paper"
Photographer: Yoshihiko Ueda

Centerfold, Outside, "Plano. Illinois"
Photographer: Yoshihiko Ueda

Centerfold, Inner Left, "Peak"
Inner Right, "Cervus canadensis (female), Cervidae"
Photographer: Yoshihiko Ueda

Final Page, "Hakkin"
Masuichi-Ichimura Sake Brewery
Photographer: Takashi Sekiguchi

060 Footprints

What is creativity? What is originality? There is a Japanese word —*jinseki-mitō*—that could be translated as "untrodden," which describes a place where humans have yet to set foot. It is both an achievement and an honor to leave one's footprints in a place so difficult to get to. One unexplored place after another has been trodden by explorers. Yet some places are still untouched—the Meili Snow Mountains in Yunnan China, for example, or Lake Vostok sleeping beneath its thick layer of Antarctic ice. The moon has been walked on by Apollo 11 commander Neil Armstrong. We have yet to reach Mars. The round trip alone would take so many years we should think carefully of the philosophical implications of sending someone to step on its surface. Still, humans yearn to leave their footprints on untouched places. Perhaps we enjoy the idea that our achievement will be literally imprinted on the land for all to see. Perhaps our image of creative inspiration is somehow linked to the adventure of reaching a place where no one else has ever walked.

Nevertheless, there can be something creative about intentionally walking on well-trodden paths. *Honkadori* in Japanese classical *waka* poetry—the technique of alluding to poems composed by one's predecessors—is creative in this sense. The idea is to lay the foundation for your own poem by quoting verbatim one or two lines from an ancient poem. In terms of true originality, this technique lacks creativity. However, honkadori aims to produce poetry based on what your readers already know. To be well grounded in waka composition, a poet must not only be skilled in conceiving new lines and phrases, he or she must also be well-grounded in the poetry of the past. It is assumed that a good waka poet knows both the poetry of his or her predecessors and the topics they depicted. The ability to compose is derived from that appreciation. Problems of universality and individuality are involved here. The notion in this poetic form is that creativity can be found when you superimpose your individuality on things that have lain within people's collective consciousness for generations.

To offer another example, imagine a tea bowl being shaped on a potter's wheel. The wheel is set on a rotor, so iterative similarities are produced naturally. You could say the tea bowl is discovered within them. In this case, creativity is found in the similarities and differences born in those rotations, even as one follows closely in another's footsteps. Many people will recognize a universal beauty here. At work is an awareness of a value transcending individual creativity, a will to purify oneself of the desire to indulge in self-expression.

At the risk of being misunderstood, I would say the type of creativity cultivated in Japanese culture does not place sole emphasis on the unexplored and untrodden. While the personal will to create is undeniably present, we embrace the attitude that, in pursuit of the universal, individuality can be relinquished. This does not mean that we strive to match up our footsteps with those who have gone before. Differences are inevitable. Thus, we show respect for the paths laid out by our forebears even as we unhesitatingly superimpose our own steps on them.

061 Concepts

Humans are conceptual beings. You can see it in our eyes. Lions do not construct concepts as they live their lives. Thus, their eyes are wild. If we did not possess words and lived by pure instinct, our eyes would be like the lion's, and we would growl from first to last. "White" is both a word and concept. Poets construct these forms of expression, leading us listeners to think about things like whiteness.

> No matter how white something is, it is not pure whiteness. Even if it shows not the slightest hint of shadow, a microscopic blackness is concealed within. That is how white is structures. White and black do not look on each other with hostility. Far from it. Rather, white produces black as a natural consequence. From the moment of its existence, whiteness constantly engenders blackness.
> —Tanikawa Shuntarō, "Personal Reflections on Ashes"

The second half of this prose poem refers to blackness in a similar manner: "No matter how black something is, it is not purely black." That is indeed the case.

If we are discussing whiteness as a concept, we must not forget the following poem.

> A white square
> Inside
> A white square
> Inside
> A white square
> Inside
> A white square
> Inside
> A white square
> —Kitasono Katsue, "Monotonous Spaces"

The poem's goal is to produce as much whiteness as possible. Newly produced white squares are born one after another inside a white square just slightly whiter than the square before it. In this case, whiteness takes on a square shape.

The imagination produced in this way is itself whiteness. Whiteness is a state from which ideas flow.

062 Synesthesia

Synesthesia is a curious perceptual phenomenon. As with, say, whiteness and milk, it is natural to associate something with white if you can visually confirm its color. But there is no physical relation between whiteness and abstract signs like mathematical figures or the alphabet. Yet I experience C as "white." A is red in my mind, B is yellow, C is white, D is blue, E is green, F is purple, G is pink. This set of associations has never changed. Among the twenty-six letters, C, H, O, and W are white. I myself do not understand why this is the case. Perhaps there is a simple explanation. Maybe colors and letters fused together because my mind is saturated with memories from primary school athletic meets, when each class was given its own colored batons and clothing. Maybe the English word "white" forged a connection with some of these letters.

Color extends beyond the universal and empirical scope of physics; it has more to do with psychology and physiology. That is, besides being governed by laws, color is a discrete process that takes place in our brains and minds. Apparently, the intensity of synesthesia differs from person to person. The most intense cases are truly impressive. For a certain individual, numbers don't just possess their own colors, they systematically arrange themselves in a linear path from one until a certain number is reached. Then—without fail—the numbers make a ninety-degree turn. I wish I could experience this first hand, but that is impossible.

Speaking of subjective experiences, the words "white person" and "black person" are also purely subjective. As colors, our images of black and brown are considerably different. Black is the darkness of the universe, while brown is the color of real-world objects. "Black people" is therefore an abstraction rather than realistic representation. This is the same with "white people." Look closely and you will see that skin is translucent. "White people" are those whose veins can be seen through their skin. "Translucent people" would thus be more fitting. When someone becomes emotionally overwrought, their faces turn red, perhaps because blood is filling the capillaries. An objective look at skin makes you realize you can't say it is white at all.

Of all the races in the world, the people whose skin I find the most translucent are the Scandinavians. Even their irises are pale. Their hair too—nowhere close to even light brown. And when you hear "blond hair" you would expect a color with some depth, but theirs is so light I wouldn't even call it blond. Perhaps Scandinavians are that color because they live at high latitudes with long winters where the weaker sun is unable to penetrate the depths of their skin. Indeed, "translucent people" is far more appropriate than "white people."

The skin color of the Scandinavian peoples looks to me like the letter L. Asian skin isn't translucent, exhibiting instead a dusky quality. Here, it is the letter J that appears the strongest.

063 Flowers

I am always struck by the beauty of white flowers.

A man named Tajima Takeo runs a paradisal private resort called the "Forest in the Sky" in Kagoshima Prefecture. Mr. Tajima once helped establish "Gajoen," another pioneering *ryokan* based on the idea of using old renovated houses and the surrounding natural topography to enchant its guests. The thatched houses were meticulously disassembled and reconstructed on the site. Then private rooms and charming, personal open-air baths were installed. A buzz surrounded Gajoen almost immediately, yet Mr. Tajima was not satisfied. He decided to make an inn that nobody could imitate. He purchased nearly twenty-five acres of a bamboo-covered mountain, clearing the land himself. Removing the dense bamboo, whose roots were tightly packed together, was numbing work. He cut them down with a chainsaw and removed them root by root leaving untouched the sawtooth and evergreen oaks and other vegetation until the mountain was reborn as a beautiful grove of mixed trees. It took six years. He worked with local carpenters to build a large wooden shelter on the massive mountain. The area saw its first use as a lunch-included outing destination for Gajoen patrons. Thus was born the Forest in the Sky resort. Another seven years passed. By then Mr. Tajima had built lodgings in areas with majestic views. Five villas dotted the mountainside, each with its own sprawling plot of land. Beyond a wooden deck lay the Kirishima Mountain Range. Enter the square onsen at the deck's edge and you feel as though you're swimming amidst the majestic panorama. To think that such an extraordinary inn is possible....

I asked Mr. Tajima what the most prized part of the resort was. He didn't miss a beat. "The smell," he said immediately. He did not mean some artificial scent. Rather, he was referring to the aroma of the surrounding farmland. Terraced fields make up part of the Forest in the Sky inn. The vegetables served at the inn are supplied by these fields. When the daikon is at its most delicious, its scent wafts up from the ground. When the celery is in season, you can smell its aroma too. Mr. Tajima calls himself "a guardian of nature"—he talks to the soil and cuts off pieces of the seasonal vegetables for their scent, placing them along the dining tables.

According to this nature-loving man, plants turn white in June. The leaves of the silver vine, for example, or Asian lizard's tail take on a bold white color that looks almost painted on. The areas that remain green on the leaves and those that turn white are easily distinguishable. From a distance you could mistake the white parts for blooming flowers. The flowers are simple and subdued. Thus, the leaves are what attracts insects to enable the plant's pollination. Mr. Tajima once told me, "I believe the phrase 'June bride' comes from this natural phenomenon." His words were persuasive, filled with the emotion of a man so close to earth and nature.

I realize now why white flowers excite me—they are luring me in! Be it flowers or leaves, their aim is to seduce the onlooker with a display of white. Of course, plants are not as white as paper. But we are tantalized by their saturated, vivid whiteness nonetheless, whether we are a honeybee or not. As living things, it is in our nature to be attracted like that.

064　Summer

Experiencing art can trigger an enormous surge of memories in our brains. These memories can be summoned by any form of artistic expression—viewing, listening, reading, etc.—that constructs an architecture of mental images. In short, our brains are made up of memories. This is what I believe.

These reawakened memories do not possess the story-like quality of "recollections." They are matter-of-fact and fragmentary. As an example, here are the images that first come to mind when I see the word *summer*: a ferry, a deck, sunlight, shadows, the sea breeze, a flag, cumulonimbus clouds, a harbor, a sandy beach, a tent, a boat, an oar, Styrofoam, ice, T-shirts, towels, a toothbrush, a breakwater, curry, soda pop, drinking glasses, rope, the shadows of fish in the water.... These images come from my high school days on Shirai, one of the Kasaoka Islands that my friends and I often visited in the Inland Sea. They run together and reconstruct an old memory that floats to the surface of my consciousness. Surely, memories formed as an adult, often involving unusual experiences or exotic travel, are far more numerous. But when it comes to familiar images like summer, it is those glistening memories of early youth we recall. Memories of the white coastal beaches of Ipanema, West Papua's coral reefs, a frigid dry martini on the counter of a Casablanca hotel bar—they may be more exciting. But when I hear "summer," the first thing I see is a pair of sand-covered sneakers. I wonder why....

Perhaps we become attached to such images in the same way we cherish the memories of our first love. Impressions deeply ingrained or burned into us when our feelings were at their most sensitive are more accessible, more secure. The search engine of our memories pulls them up first, perhaps. The emotional structures we developed as babies and children are like sponges. Even the most commonplace experience—indeed, everything—is irresistibly absorbed into them and kept in permanent, unmoving layers.

Memories, like unorganized collections of data, do not line up neatly in our minds. Instead, they form multiplicities of hyperlink-like connections. They form the background of every image, every reaction. A child perceives the world by crawling about, putting everything he can into his mouth to taste. Even if we do not put, say, a brush into our mouths, we can predict with almost perfect accuracy what its bristles would feel like. This must be because analogous experiences are stored up in our minds as memory chains. If that is the case, there must be portions of my memory connected to underlying layers of personal history. In other words, the environment of Okayama Prefecture —where I was born and raised—and the memories I amassed there must form the basis of the way I experience the world.

Perhaps I experience "white" when I hear "summer" because of that same mechanism.

065 Hakkin

I once designed a sake bottle with a stainless-steel, mirror-like surface. But it didn't taper off at the top like sake bottles usually do. I designed it to feel somewhat small, like a slim brick placed vertically. If the typical, sloping-shouldered bottle looks like a crane, then mine looks like an owl with its head tucked in to sleep. My bottle's shape is like the cross section of an ellipse, rising in a perfectly straight line, then rounding out at the top like a bottle of Bordeaux. The neck is short, about one-third that of a wine bottle. To close the bottle, I decided on a small round cap shaped like a go stone that fits snugly into the top. The bottle has a shiny, mirror-like surface—not even a label blemishes it. A long, thin washi seal strip is pasted over the go-shaped cap from rear to front. The tiny label is tightly rolled over the short bottleneck and fixed in place.

The paper seal is hand-torn. That is, it has rough edges, not the sharp edges of a machine-cut piece of paper. The characters for "Hakkin"—in Japanese, "white gold"—are written in black on the small seal. The bottle deviates radically from a conventional sake shape and materials. I feel, however, that the bottle responds to the Japanese sake inside, for the design is based on the impression one gets from the emptiness of a mirror.

That sake is produced by the long-established Nagano chestnut sweet shop called Obusedō, which, aside from making confectionery, also runs a sake brewery called Masuichi-Ichimura. This is high-quality sake made in limited amounts. Yet Obusedō is not only a chestnut sweet shop and sake brewery. Rather, it is an entire neighborhood complex, a microcosm, you could say—a blending together of a confectionary factory, a Western-style restaurant, an inn, a tea house, a bar, a club restaurant, a garden for growing large metasequoia trees, and a series of pathways with paving blocks of hard chestnut wood.

The complex even has a magnificent Katsushika Hokusai art museum. Takai Kōzan, who once led the entire institution, was a patron and friend of the artist. In ages past, there was a tradition called *danna* culture in Japan: a danna, a wealthy merchant or industrialist with a highly developed aesthetic sense—Takai Kōzan fits the description perfectly—would sponsor talented craftspeople and artists to offer their artistic skills to create various daily necessities, housing, gardens, chimneys, and the like. Hokusai came to the area from Edo as part of this artistic movement, and stayed, spending the rest of his life in the town.

In the 1990s the American Sarah Marie Cummings, realizing the potential for this location, which she sensed was a crucible of Japanese culture, expended an incredible amount of effort on behalf of the Obusedō administration committee. From time to time, a person from a foreign country recognizes the virtue of a cultural asset even better than those within that culture. Yet Sarah's vision extended beyond even this. She saw the future of Obusedō, too. My Hakkin sake bottles were commissioned by Sarah, the wonder that she is.

She is no longer there, yet her traces remain in the sake brewing scenes and illustrations that cover the Masuichi-Ichimura Brewery walls, where a Caucasian woman with blonde hair and blue eyes wearing the Masuichi livery directs the brewery workers. The stainless-steel bottle derives from those circumstances. The story took place long ago, but the light from this "Hakkin" bottle just grows brighter as time goes by.

066 Hakkaisan

> The train came out of the long tunnel, crossing into the realm
> of the snow country. The night was white to its core.

Thus begins Kawabata Yasunari's novel *Snow Country*. The phrase
"The night was white to its core" makes me wonder what the surrounding environment must have looked like. At a time when the
night was much darker than today, under a black and starless sky and
with so few artificial lights, the snow must have covered everything as
far as the eye could see. The core of the night's darkness may indeed
be a pale white. The novel is set in the town of Yuzawa, the setting for
a tale that takes place in a hot spring spa.

Minamiuonuma, the town adjacent to Yuzawa, experiences
some of the heaviest snowfall in Japan. It was also once known for
its rice. Mount Hakkai's towering ridge connects the multilayered
peaks and crests of the area. A sake called "Hakkaisan" is made
using the super-soft water—called "the water of thunder and light-
ning"—that gushes out of its geological namesake Mount Hakkai.
For many years now, I have helped the company construct this
sake's image. I help with designing bottles and labels, of course.
But when it comes to expressing the value of the sake itself, the
challenge is to convey as clearly as possible its relation to its
natural environment.

In general, there are two kinds of sake: one that is produced
in massive amounts with quantity as its goal, and the other, made in
small amounts, that strives for quality. The first is good sake that you
can drink in a lively, comfortable way; the second aims to deepen its
connection to the food it accompanies and explore subtle differences
in flavor. It's not a question of which is better, but simply that Mount
Hakkai stands proudly as an example of the latter kind.

Today, using its nature, topography, culture, and cuisine as resources, Japan welcomes visitors from an ever-widening world. We are entering an era in which we must better understand how to explain and offer to foreign eyes the value we know exists in these resources and nowhere else. When it comes to Hakkaisan sake—named after one of the three mountains of Echigo—we must do more than simply extol the sake; we must also interpret and illuminate the potential of the climate, geography, and food culture of the region.

Minamiuonuma is often blanketed by snow, which falls so thickly that even the eaves of houses disappear. This is not your typical snow either. Winds filled with moisture are pushed upwards after colliding with the region's high mountains. The air is chilled, and the moisture falls as snow. Niigata Prefecture's heavy snow makes it unusually well equipped to deal with this environment. Furthermore, as an area adjacent to the hot springs resort depicted in Snow Country, the steaming baths of Minamiuonuma suit the snowy scenery. Koshihikari rice, chewy yet moist, is grown here. The extreme shifts in temperature from day to night make this long-admired rice utterly delicious. Hakkaisan sake fully embodies these topographical features and products.

France's Bordeaux is a symbol of red wine. This is not only due to its flavor. Wineries that were once the castles of feudal lords dot a landscape of breathtaking vineyards, a uniquely beautiful scenery that is evoked in the wine itself. How to evoke a region of rice, snow, and steam in a bottle of sake? The challenge makes me quiver with excitement.

067 Koshu

There is a white wine made from a type of Japan-grown grape. The wine is called Koshu, named directly after that grape. It is made by the Central Wine, Ltd. winery company based in Katsunuma and Hokuto in Yamanashi Prefecture and led by Misawa Shigekazu, a man with a burning passion for wine-making. Through an intermediary, I was tasked with designing his company's wine label.

This light, refreshing wine once carried a French-style label. This struck me as a shame. I considered it a shallow gesture that pandered to preconceptions about wine. If it was to enter the world arena, this Japanese wine would have to reflect the place it came from. To assume that a global spirit must necessarily be occidental is to mistake an effect for the cause. To face the world, a place must express its own here and now; if it imitates others it will be ignored. Undoubtedly, the essence of any culture lies within the particularities of the land.

Thus, I designed a label with the name Koshu displayed in vivid black calligraphy on the front. I remember this was just before the year 2000. At first, the wine-makers received the opposite advice from a sommelier they consulted—that is, to make the label more "French." But I was allowed to reject this advice. I opted for a woodblock printing technique to give the label a sense of maturity. I then intentionally arranged the characters of the word unevenly to produce a unique tone. The result was initially considered "messy," and a number of people apparently complained. Yet, they slowly came to understand that the label—with its asymmetrical features and large blank spaces—was emblematic of the quality of the bottle's contents.

The wine—made to be lighter and smoother than even a Chardonnay—is an exquisite companion for delicate foods like thin slices of flounder sprinkled with *tachibana* citrus vinegar and salt. Ever since the *umami*-based flavors of Japanese-style cooking began influencing the world's chefs, Koshu wine has drawn international attention, winning one first-place prize after another at well-known wine competitions. Europe was the birthplace of wine, so it is inevitable that European wine is prized around the world. Yet Koshu wine complements just about anything. It is under this banner that the wine has found a secure place on the world stage.

Despite his stubbornness, Misawa Shigekazu is a man willing to solicit help. When critical comments arise, he responds by improving the quality of the wine and upgrading the winery's facilities. Alcohol's charms are not exclusively for the tongue. No matter how many times they are told, people tend not to get the message that a winery's equipment, and its surrounding scenery, are vital to the winemaking process. But in the end, that is probably just fine. You cannot get by in this world with talent alone. The stubbornness of a Mr. Misawa is essential, but so is patience. I believe that what we come to care for most is cultivated in this way. Capitalism may soon face its demise, but the value created by an earnest desire to succeed will survive in whatever context or time. It is to engage with just such an attitude that I continue to design.

068 Baijiu

Toasting in China differs from that of Japan. You must drain your entire cup and, as proof, turn it upside down for all to see. The drink used in toasts is a transparent, high-proof liquor called *baijiu*—literally, white alcohol. It is distilled from the kaoliang plant and has an average alcohol content of over 50 percent. Because of this, a toasting glass is a relatively small, thick glass cup. If you want to make friends with someone, baijiu will get you there in no time—you eat and drink cup after cup together until you are both drunk. You need to be especially careful, however, of the size of the round table you sit at. Sitting with seven or eight people is no problem. But when you sit around a table of twenty or more, you will need strong determination. You must engage head on with your hosts and fellow guests, every one of whom will rise with a full glass in hand. One after another they bear down on you like a squadron of approaching bombers, with volley after volley of toasts. As soon as you gulp one drink, your baijiu cup is immediately refilled, and the next guest is in front of you, smiling from ear to ear. You drink the glass dry and turn it upside down. This cycle repeats over and over as the party plays out.

Recently, in cities like Beijing and Shanghai, drinking customs have loosened somewhat. But they are still going strong in places like Sichuan and its surrounding provinces. You will gulp down baijiu and gorge yourselves with their famous "hot pot," all the while deepening your friendships. Sichuan food is famous for its spiciness even within Chinese cuisine, and a high-proof baijiu complements it nicely.

There are various kinds of spiciness. The brininess of salt and soy sauce, the smoldering heat of chili peppers, the pleasing sharpness of black pepper, the pungency of wasabi, the numbing heat of sanshō pepper.... The spice that gives Sichuan hot pot its heat is *mala*—a fusion of *sanshō* with chili pepper that leaves a sharp, numbing sensation on your tongue.

Hot pot is truly the crucible of mala. Like *shabu-shabu*, you throw meat or vegetables into a boiling pot of soup. Once they have cooked through, you take the now soup-flavoured items and dip them in a special sauce before eating. The round *nabe* pot looks like a yin-yang symbol, separated by a curved divider into two sections—one side containing a dark red soup, the other a cloudy white one. But this is no transparent *dashi* broth. Chili peppers and sanshō float close together in the dark red soup, so it is already quite spicy. Then, you take the piping hot items and dip them into a *tare* sauce, which can be a mixture of red chili oil and minced garlic, or sesame seed oil and finely sliced spring onions, or a thick *jiang* sauce filled with cilantro. Each sauce has a different type of spiciness, so your mouth inevitably flares up with the incredible heat. This is where the baijiu comes in. This high-proof, transparent alcohol is able to compete with the fiery spices and oils. Its role is to neatly wash down and soothe their powers.

The inside of the boiling pot is already a flaming hell. Nevertheless, we go to the extreme and make our food still more spicy by dipping it in the tare. I see something characteristically human about this. Using the biting baijiu to combine all the intensities of the food is the epitome of Sichuan cooking. The mixing of mala and baijiu makes one's tongue, which is already numb from the back-to-back toasts, even more numb. Yet, before you know it, you just can't get enough.

069 Makgeolli

Sake demands to be offered generously. In the world of Japanese sake, a kind called *daiginjō* has recently been gathering attention. It is a top-quality sake made from brewer's rice milled down to 50 percent of its original weight. These days, people also place emphasis on a sake's aroma and general level of perfection. Still, it is difficult to ignore the attraction of going to an *izakaya* and sitting down to a friendly and familiar cup of completely ordinary *junmai*—that is, sake without any milling requirements at all. I am unsure when the custom was established, but sake is sometimes served in a glass placed on top of a saucer. The liquid is intentionally allowed to overflow generously as it pours from the bottle, so that it spills into the saucer. Only then is the sake offered. The saucer itself, sometimes a box of cypress wood, holds about 180 milliliters and the overflowing sake fills it to the brim. You gently lift the saucer and bring your mouth down to meet it so as not to spill the quivering contents, curving up toward you ever so slightly from the surface tension. What a lavish way to serve and savor sake!

Travelling through Europe you encounter wine glasses and beer mugs with volume lines marked on them. This apparently relates to a regulation stating that the beverage should be poured up to the line to ensure customers are not swindled. Yet what a crass way to serve alcohol! Asian cultures are by and large more tolerant of common folk who desire to plunge into the world of drunkenness. Prearranging the amount of alcohol to craftily turn a profit is stingy and shameful no matter how you slice it. There must be some tacit agreement at work here.

In our neighboring country, Korea, a traditional alcoholic drink called *makgeolli* is gaining popularity among young people. Like the Japanese nigori sake, makgeolli is a cloudy white, unfiltered rice wine, from which the sediment that accumulates during the brewing process is not removed. Its alcohol content is closer to beer than sake, so it goes down smooth. In the past, it seems, makgeolli was drunk almost exclusively in agricultural areas, something farmers would partake of during rainy days when their farm work was put on hold. Apparently, many elderly Koreans say they still yearn for some whenever it rains. But the young enjoy it almost exclusively as a casual drink during meals.

You ladle the makgeolli into large, bowl-like serving cups from an earthenware jar using a spoon that looks like a gourd split in half. This is very satisfying as the cups hold ample amounts of the drink. Makgeolli pairs nicely with dishes that contain thinly sliced, grilled pork or Korean *buchimgae* pancake. I have even seen it served in a large brass kettle at a place that offers these foods. It was a skillfully crafted, rough-faced kettle not unlike those once used to sprinkle water over concussed rugby players to revive them on the field, and so big you might hesitate to lug it out to the dining table. Nevertheless, I was deeply impressed with the way it lent itself to the spirit of serving up alcohol.

Pour the makgeolli into a large, bowl-like Joseon *hakuji* cup. You will clearly see its cloudy whiteness. The somewhat sour, ever-so-slightly carbonated taste—I feel nostalgic for Korea's magnanimous drink.

070 The Palm of the Hand

I gently open my hands. I feel the whiteness of their palms. To think what humanity has made with these soft hands.... That history is about to end.

In 2016, I held an exhibition called "Neo-Prehistory—100 Verbs" in Milan. The design of the exhibition was as follows: I selected one hundred tools, from the Stone Age to the present, and displayed them alongside corresponding verbs. The overarching theme of the verbs was desire. Human history—with its religions, ideologies, politics, and technologies—is a complex fabric with innumerable strands in its warp and weft. I wanted to pull on these various threads to draw out a simplified history of desire.

The first item is an unworked stone. The accompanying verb is *Exist*. The world began with a sense of what it is simply to exist. The second is a stone tool dating from the earliest tool-making phase of human life. The verb: *Hold*. When the hand encountered the stone, the stone taught the hand what it meant to hold. The multiplying meanings of the tools continues with *Destroy, Strike, Crush, Make, Kill, Improve, Shoot,* etc. When two phenomena are said to "coevolve," it means each evolves while exerting an influence on the other. Tools coevolved with our desires, and they continue to do so to this day. Such is the history that humanity weaves.

The verbs continue with *Fear* and *Worship*, marking our reverence for nature and the universe. Then, *Save* and *Divide*, referring to activities that paved the way for agriculture and settlements—fuses that ignited the rapid evolution of tools and desires. Gunpowder, paper, and the compass throw open the doors of desire still further, bringing in new ambitions in the form of astronomy and physics. Conflict between cultures erupts, and the emotions that drive us to violate and dominate are also forged, alongside the development of tools that immeasurably expand the potential for destruction. Eventually, we reach the atomic bomb; we reach *Despair.*

Most of the items on display were gathered with the help of the many art galleries and museums in Italy. They reproduced exact scale models of the screws used on the Titanic, over nine meters in diameter, the atomic bomb dropped on Hiroshima ("Little Boy"), a Tomahawk cruise missile, and many other items.

Evolution is not all about accumulating wisdom. Foolishness, cruelty, and cunning also evolve. By clinging to the concept "I" for generation after generation, humans have destroyed their environment and violated their neighbors. Learning nothing from this, we continue to consume enormous quantities of fossil fuels while roaming the earth.

Computers, spaceships, and mobile telephones are all products of the twentieth century. New tools are already taking shape as we progress through the twenty-first. The verbs *Recycle, Self-organize, Operate by remote control, Microminiaturize* and the like hint that the era we are living through is rampant with new, complex desires.

The final exhibition item was a hologram of a to-scale heart beating in mid-air. The title verb is *Regenerate.* The exhibition-goers hear a low, pulsing thump-thump, thump-thump from the moment they arrive in the hall until they finally arrive at the regenerated heart.

With artificial intelligence in the palm of our hand, humanity once again stands at the brink of a new dawn. I once again gently open my hands.

071 The Sole of the Foot

The sole of the foot is white. The palms and soles of black people appear even whiter. This is also true of white and yellow people, but it is less conspicuous since the contrast is less. Standing and walking upright are natural to us now, but they are in fact difficult feats. A cat, with its quick reflexes, would surely break into a two-legged run when it needed to, if it could. But, in the end, such a thing is not feasible. Only in picture books and fairy-tales do we encounter Puss in Boots. Walking upright is abnormal for every other animal. Only we can do it.

It is said that humans became bipeds when we climbed down from our lives in the trees to walk the surface of the earth. Indeed, there is nothing for toes to grasp on a flat plain. And if your goal is to gain a better perspective by lifting your eyes higher, then standing is the best approach. The gravitational force of the earth supported this transformation, and the ground was firm enough to support the weight of a human body. We cannot stand on a swamp or an ocean, but we certainly can on land.

When we acquired the ability to stand, our points of contact with the ground came to be the soles of our feet. But it is only recently that we began wearing shoes. Australopithecus first walked upright four million years ago, while only a few thousand years have passed since we began to cover our feet. Tutankhamen of Egypt wore golden sandals. The 5,300-year-old "Iceman" found at the border of Italy and Austria wore leather shoes. Before that, however, we walked barefoot on the earth. I imagine our bare soles conveyed various kinds of information from the ground—important information. They could feel moisture levels, the hardness or softness of the ground. They could also help determine if digging in a certain area would lead to water or if earthworms were likely to be found, the kind of thing that was not only useful but connected to matters of life and death. We interacted with our environment this way, perceiving with the soles of our feet minute differences in the condition of the ground.

It was at an old hotel in Bali that I first came to be impressed by how pleasant it is to notice what the feet feel. This was a long-established hotel which had a group of cottages scattered over a large plot of land. Large stones were set into the sort of pathways you might find in a plaza. The stones' surfaces were worn down from being trodden over many years. They imparted a comfort like no other, as if the stones were made for my feet. I greatly enjoyed their smooth, curved surfaces. One would think that the uneven undulations have thrown me off—too much information. But my soles responded to every step.

We may sense, however faintly, that our white soles were once our most active sensory antennae. Yet now they tend to be sealed in layers of shoe and sock.

072 Eyes

To say, "to open one's eyes wide in fear or anger" in the Japanese language is "to peel the whites of the eyes," while "to look coldly at" is "to look at someone with white eyes." They are not the most pleasant phrases, no matter how you parse them. The dark center of the eye, the pupil, functions to regulate amounts of light, but it also widens when we see something that pleases or intrigues us. When we say that large, dark eyes are beautiful, we unconsciously refer to eyes with dilated pupils; they leave a favorable impression. If, on the other hand, someone looks at us with annoyance, finding us uninteresting or somehow disagreeable, their pupils contract. Perhaps this is why, when people's eyes appear overly white, we interpret their gaze as cold and unfeeling. Thus, we do not want to be looked at with "white eyes."

But what if eyes were completely black? Their capacity for expression would obviously be lost and they would be unable to communicate any kind of mutual understanding. You would be looking into the eyes of an alien. You would be left to wonder what they were thinking and feeling. Our expectation that if we look into someone's eyes we can read their feelings means we can see warmth, but also coldness there. Our unease about the gaze of others would be worse if their eyes were completely black.

The eyes say more than the mouth. If you and someone else lock eyes, you can carry on an entire dialogue by subtly altering your expressions. Not all of the changes in our moods and internal states can be expressed through the blunt instruments of words. Our spirits constantly vibrate within us. We live with those minute tremblings. Eyes convey those feelings very clearly. Eye contact directs one's most delicate sensors towards the other. I have no doubt that an overflowing compassion can stem from this act. It follows that the whites of the eyes are an indispensable background that brings into relief the expressive changes of the pupil. When we perceive the world with our eyes, we also sending signals about those perceptions to others. We "speak" quickly, even loquaciously, through those same eyes. We live our lives unconsciously reacting to eyes' shifting messages.

I once stood completely alone in the middle of a Mongolian plain under a starless jet-black sky. We had three tiny yurts lined up together in a vast land, an expanse so perfectly flat you could see nothing but the horizon. I bedded down by myself, but in the dead of night, I felt a strange presence. I decided to step outside my yurt, only to find the darkness was full of innumerable bright eyes looking at me. I was so surprised I was stunned into silence. But when I calmed down and took a better look, I realized they were the eyes of grazing sheep who had gathered in the area surrounding the yurts. It was at that moment that I realized eyes give off light.

I was taught that the eye is a sense organ designed for seeing, but perhaps it is better described as an organ in which something valuable can be seen. Such are the thoughts that come to me when looking at my own eyes in the mirror.

073 Gradual Changes

Why does our hair turn white? Put crudely, it's aging, of course. But why does it happen to hair that was once deep black? Perhaps because white marks the boundary between life and death; it signifies that we are approaching that other place.

I had a lot of hair when I was young. When did white hair start springing from my head? Perhaps it was just after I had turned twenty. I remember I was on a date with my girlfriend. I had laid my head on her lap while we sat on a lawn so that she could pluck out white hairs for me. I remember she had to search for some time before finding one, so I must not have had that many. This hair-plucking girlfriend would eventually become my wife. It didn't take long, though, to reach the point where she refused to do it for me. The white strands were so many it would have been unfair of me to insist. Not only would it have been troublesome to remove all those hairs, it might well have come out in clumps, leaving me with far too little. I remember finally accepting it, saying, "I guess I'm stuck with a white head of hair!"

When half your hair turns white, it is called "silver-gray hair" —or in Japanese, "romance gray." But what exactly does this romance mean? Perhaps it suggests the lingering longing for romance in an older man already moving away from such things. Or perhaps someone hit the nail on the head when they said it referred to the reluctance to give up one's youth. Or maybe romance gray is the point at which an older man's dulling senses and slower responses are mistaken for a tolerant open-mindedness—those moments when he appears to be a great guy.

From the moment one's hair turns gray, the strands are already almost pure white. It is no longer a matter of asking someone to pluck them out. White hair not only has a distinct color; it also has a certain feel, a certain stiffness, a certain waviness. These make it unlike the original, black, flexible hair. Somewhat inflexible, slightly hard, wavy white hairs pop up all over the head. Of course, everyone is different. But that is how my hair turned out. Once this happens, you have to take a so-what attitude towards the situation. You feel that, like the face you were born with, there really is nothing you can do about the way your hair is changing. As I wrote in a previous entry, all my clothes are black. I travel a lot for work, so for convenience's sake I simply prepare the same colored shirts, pants, and socks for each day I am going to be away. I know this is a bit too relaxed. However, since my hair has become messy and white, I have become resigned to my fate. I figure my hair and my clothes are just part of my image now.

I have my hair cut once a month. Looking at the floor, I am surprised to see there are still some black hairs left. They somehow make me feel I still have more dues to pay, more knowledge to gain. I think to myself, "I've got to make my hair whiter!"

074 Powder

Matter mainly takes the form of a solid, a liquid, or a gas, but there are a few other forms too, one of which is powder, that is, a "particulate." It behaves differently from all the other forms. It is made up of particles and grains, which, when magnified, are seen to be solid. Yet when these come together as a powder—which includes an intermediary empty space interposed between the particles—the compound has physical properties that are unlike any other solid.

An hourglass is a perfect example. If its contents were a true solid, no particles would drop down. Were it a liquid, surface tension would prevent the liquid from slipping through the narrow hole. Sand passes through, however, since it is made of perfectly sized, tiny grains. Because these particles are minerals with an appropriate weight, they flow through the narrow opening, rather than jamming it. When you magnify this, you see an unvarying volume of grains tumbling through the aperture. The hourglass can measure a fixed amount of time precisely because this phenomenon is so constant.

There are places like the Sahara Desert where enormous amounts of particulate have collected. Sand dunes that look like swelling waves stretch to the horizon, their surface covered in beautiful ripples shaped by the wind. Such a scene is astonishing; it can leave you speechless. Over unimaginable periods of time, rocks turn to pebbles, pebbles to sand, and sand to a homogeneous dust. Faced by such a blinding landscape and the unbelievably large amount of intermingled sediment, some people are struck by the transience of mortal life, while others are overcome by a sudden hopelessness.

Deserts migrate, propelled by the wind. The grains of Sahara sand are tiny because they are worn down by the desert's perpetual movement. Scoop it up in your hand and toss it away. Rather than falling, it scatters and disappears along with its shadow. Despite being so minute, however, each grain is a mineral with a specific weight. Thus, they are governed by physical laws that produce the dunes' wavelike undulations.

Powder will form a cone when poured carefully onto a soft surface from a height; that is, it will take the shape of a mountain. Pour more sand, and the mountain increases its size but maintains its congruent shape. This mountain's constant, stable angle of inclination is apparently called "the angle of repose." This angle changes depending on the size, weight, and frictional coefficient of the particles. The sands of the Sahara take the magnificent shape they do because the uniformly sized grains of sand sustain a specific angle of repose. Subtle patterns are engraved as the wind passes over that surface. Because these exquisite shapes are produced by a physics-based equilibrium, they are destroyed when anybody walks along the edge of the dune; the result is a collapse of sand not unlike the sweep of an avalanche, spreading out for a surprising distance.

The moment you find a small pile of powder under the paper wrapper of powdered medicine, or touch with your fingertips the white powder clinging to the surface of a *daifuku-mochi*, you are feeling the presence of the mechanics hidden within these powders. It is, we can sense, the breath of the universe made concrete.

075 Corners

A sheet of paper is white and taut, but it does not spread out infinitely in all directions. It necessarily has four edges and four tips. And it takes on a whole other life in those four tips, that is, those four corners.

In ages past, when paper was made by hand, its size was determined by the proportions of the paper-making screen, a mat-like tool made of cypress wood. In this process, the portion of the paper-pulp that met the edges of the screen remained on the final product as a deckled edge called the "ear" of the sheet. This ear has an elegant air, but if the paper was to be used for writing thank you notes, this ear was cut off, leaving a smart, four-cornered page.

With machines, the width of the paper is predetermined, while the length is not: at least in principle, it can be made as long as you like. Ordinarily, a pre-defined amount is rolled up, cut, then distributed. In this case, too, the ear that forms on the side of the paper is cut away leaving a rectangular sheet. Paper's aspect ratio is $1:\sqrt{2}$. Cutting it in half—even cutting this half in half—will not change this ratio.

When using paper, the most fragile areas are the corners—the Achilles heel of any quadrilateral. When we sit up straight to handle an important certificate, good stationery, or a business card, we are responding to the neat, precise shape of the corners. A new banknote also has this uniquely bracing effect. Gift bags and wrapped packages whose corners are neatly folded are also far more satisfying. In such ways do we unconsciously pay attention to corners.

You can convey a sincere feeling of hospitality to a guest by simply placing a pristine sheet of white paper on a black tray. You can mark the significance of a tensely negotiated contract or settlement by proffering the crucial documents in an unblemished envelope. If the paper we use for tea ceremony sweets or the notepaper on which we write personal messages did not have four clean corners, they would feel insincere.

Yet corners are fragile and easily damaged. Blemishes are immediately noticed. Indeed, people's emotions are invested in protecting corners. But no matter how careful you are, it is impossible to preserve the sharp points of corners indefinitely. Business cards become rounded in our pockets. The banknotes in our wallets slowly wrinkle. Our receipts crumple almost right away. When we look at a postcard's corners, we can see the journey it took through time and space as well as the hands that touched it on its way.

This pattern carries over to books. The corners of the pages of a recently printed book—pages for the body of the text, the introduction, the cover—look as if they shine with a dazzling light. As time passes and the book passes through multiple hands, it becomes shabby. But I think people find this wear and tear endearing.

Paper reflects people's sensibilities. Perhaps we unconsciously associate the condition of its corners with our own inner states and our gradually changing bodies.

076 Protein

Heat an egg and it will solidify, but it does not do so uniformly. I sprinkle finely cut pieces of bacon over a well-browned, lightly buttered slice of toast. I then strike off the top of a soft-boiled egg with a spoon and spread the contents out to the toast's edges. I open my mouth as wide as possible while eating, so as not to spill any of it. When traveling in Europe, I don't feel right unless I eat this for breakfast. Furthermore, I feel uncomfortable if the egg is not soft-boiled the way I like it. Browning the toast is easy. You can check it at any time whether it's a pop-up or a conveyer toaster, so there really is nothing to worry about. The real issue is how long to boil the egg.

If you are at home using a familiar pot you can simply time the process. But for some reason, my desire to cook an egg for myself disappears if I am anywhere else. Instead I look for a perfect egg at a restaurant near my hotel. Most hotels rooms are equipped with the utensils needed to boil an egg. Using a long-handled wire mesh spoon just large enough for an egg, place the egg in an electric kettle that has come to a boil. Hang the spoon's hooked handle on the edge of the pot. Six minutes on your smartphone timer. Taking care not to burn your fingertips on the pot, transfer the egg to an eggcup and carry it to your table. The entire process will take several minutes, but stay with it, do not lose focus. You might mistakenly misplace the all-important egg while rummaging around for something else. You might absentmindedly switch off the electric kettle. These things happen. But then again, one does feel silly standing next to the pot watching the water boil.

Now, take the piping hot egg and tap the top with a spoon until it cracks. Then slowly peel away the shell. It is crucial to do this in a clean, tidy way. Successfully peeling away that thin layer of semi-transparent skin between the shell and the egg white is a deeply satisfying feeling. When the smooth, steaming white top peeks through, it is a moment of pure bliss. Sprinkling salt and pepper on that small area is fulfilling too. Salt and pepper are excellent in the dry European air. Scoop out the perfectly solidified white protein with a silver spoon and the yolk will make its appearance. It is of paramount importance that you make sure the yolk has reached the ideal soft-boiled state. You get more consistent results if you carefully lower a room-temperature egg into boiling water than if you place it in cool water and then bring it to a boil. If others are also boiling eggs and you mistake your egg for someone else's, though, the game is over. You can distinguish whose is whose by the slight shift in appearance when the cooked white starts to show through the shell. The disappointment when an overcooked, pale yellow yolk peeks out of hard egg white, instead of the darker, glistening half-cooked yolk dribbling from soft egg white.... Well, small frustrations such as that are a sad part of life.

The ideal solid protein.... A great day begins with this small happiness.

077 Squid

What if there was no such thing as squid sushi? You might think *nigiri* toppings are chosen solely for their flavors, but appearance and color are equally important. Squid, especially compared to the numerous other sushi toppings, is white. I once asked a chef, "Why is squid white? While it's alive it's semi-transparent!" "Well, after some time passes the squid will just turn white," was the answer. Apparently, this is how to tell if the squid is fresh enough for nigiri. Squid turns white over time. White squid does a fine job on sushi.

There is no one way to eat sushi. Keeping the season in mind, you can ask for a chef's recommendations and order some of the ones you like. Somehow, you will always end up coming across something you are already intimately familiar with. White-fleshed fish like flounder or sea bream are served first, followed by shiny fish like pilchard or horse mackerel, until you finally reach fatty tuna or sea urchin. The meal closes with sweeter toppings like conger eel or egg. Yet part of sushi's allure is in those unexpected entrances or deviations. For example, instead of wasabi on the opening white-fleshed fish, add salt. Or if it's summer, *tachibana* citrus vinegar. Surprises like these fill one's empty stomach with joy.

Sake works well here, too. Served hot, cold, or at room temperature, it fuses and binds with the amino acids in the fish, bringing out their *umami* flavor. Perhaps this is why the drink is so appropriate for Japanese-style meals. On the other hand, a new white wine made from Japanese grapes is extremely smooth and even more refreshing than a dry Chardonnay. It further refines the flavor of the white-fleshed fish nigiri that starts the meal. With the wine, however, the sushi rice somehow starts to feel in the way. So, from the middle of the meal onward, I do away with the nigiri and instead linger over sashimi courses, sampling the various fish as I like.

And then comes the squid. The consistency of squid nigiri changes drastically depending on the way it is cut. With this topping in particular, one should defer to the skills of a chef. However, if I feel I would like to sustain the effects of the wine, which has just started kicking in, for just a little longer, I continue with the other sashimi. Indeed, in this case, semi-transparent squid is best. At such times, an attentive chef will, without a word, offer up grilled squid legs and the like. Cooked squid has a sweet whiteness and unique texture. Thus, I feel particularly well looked after when a chef offers this enjoyable and surprising delicacy.

In another context, when sushi is served on an *oke*—a large, circular, black-lacquered or cypress-wood serving platter—squid's whiteness sets off the other colors in a most satisfying way. The different hues are like an artist's palette of raw fish. The whiteness of squid restrains the loud colors of the fish, giving the near-to-overflowing oke a somewhat intellectual air. The artistry of such an arrangement makes me think, "Don't mind if I do!"

Squid is eaten around the world, and large amounts are caught even today. It may not be a perennial favorite, but I feel squid somehow makes the world a more peaceful place.

078　Whitebait

My friend from Kōchi Prefecture once sent me whitebait saying, "Here's a present of twenty thousand whole fish!" I received the gift happily, grateful to have a friend kind enough to send me these treasures from his hometown, and grateful also for his characteristic sense of humor. How many grains of cooked rice fit inside a bowl? People say there are three hundred grains in each piece of *nigiri* sushi. So, would that make one thousand per bowl? Pile on top of your steaming, thousand-grained heap an equal number of whitebait and shovel a bite into your mouth. Pure bliss.

I have already mentioned Yoshida Keisuku in a previous entry. Mr. Yoshida was taught by Yanagi Sōetsu and Serizawa Keisuke, core figures in the Folk Art Movement. He founded the Keijusha *washi* production company in Yatsuo, Toyama Prefecture. He also reconstructed an old elementary school building in a corner of his property and set up an exhibit of cultural objects related to washi that he called the Washi Library. His life of backbreaking, hard work sent strong roots deep into the earth for all of us. He passed away in 2014 at ninety-nine. In life, he supported Yatsuo's Kaze no Bon festival and quietly filled all his endeavors with Japanese beauty. That beauty still lives on today.

The man who sent me twenty thousand fish is the designer Umebara Makoto. He sent the same gift to Yoshida Keisuku, who sent back a letter of thanks that said, "It would be a shame to receive such a delicious gift only once! By all means, send another batch." Umebara was understandably blown away by Mr. Yoshida's unique way of expressing joy and gratitude. Each gesture—sending twenty thousand fish on the one hand and asking for another twenty thousand by way of gratitude, on the other—in its own way typifies the toughness of the Japanese spirit.

Among the essays that Mr. Yoshida wrote, one particular piece always comes to mind. It recounts an experience he had during the war. He was asked by the successor of *Tama*, a *tanka* magazine founded and run by Kitahara Hakushū, to take bundles of notebooks containing Hakushū's poetry away from Tokyo, where the air raids were intensifying, to Shinshū Prefecture—now Nagano Prefecture—where Hakushū's younger sister lived with her family. The bundles weighed a ton, and were so large they filled the better part of a suitcase. Mr. Yoshida's memories of the event began when he stopped at a friend's house along the way to replace all the cords around the bundles, which looked as if they would break at any moment. It was not until then that Mr. Yoshida actually saw the notebooks, which he discovered were all written in pencil. The pages were so full of layered revisions —erasing and rewriting, erasing and rewriting—that they were almost impossible to read. Mr. Yoshida was deeply impressed by the fact that even a poet as great as Hakushū was prone to hesitation. He realized that he had to take the notebooks to the safety of Shinshū no matter what. After spending that night on a packed train, he exited alone at a small station called Ōya and set out on foot. The heavy bag dug into his hand, but he bore the pain until he finally delivered the package to its destination, a cozy house with a thatched roof. A mild-mannered woman thanked him and invited him in for a breakfast of piping hot miso soup and pure white rice. He was served a white rice meal at a time when rice was usually mixed with sweet potato stems and the like. "This is surely the epitome of hospitality," he mused.

For some reason, this anecdote popped into my head when I received the twenty thousand fish. When I imagined Yoshida Keisuku eating his mountain of whitebait and rice, I found myself feeling very happy.

079 Plain Wood

Plain wood—literally in the Japanese, "white" wood—is a raw material unique to Japanese housing. It refers to unfinished wood, left just as it is after the bark has been stripped. Because it comes from bright-complexioned conifers like hinoki cypress and Japanese cedar, white wood is often assumed to refer to the color of the lumber. But this whiteness isn't a "color." The term simply refers to a bare untreated wood.

In contemporary architecture, it is normal to leave large open spaces behind rafters and beams in the ceiling. But in traditional architecture, everything was sealed up with earth, so any timber used had to be covered. To expose the faces of the pillars and beams as wooden end-sections in the completed structures, therefore, countless framing styles and methods had to be devised to turn those long pieces of wood into beautiful, handsome buildings. Nowadays, perhaps, we can only admire the beauty of plain wood when we look at the counters of sushi restaurants. Remnants of this aesthetic, however, can also still be found in Japanese fences, doors, lattices, and *agarikamachi* thresholds. In other words, you can experience the multifaceted beauty of wood merely by entering your home. You can also feel the delicacy of plain wood when you venture further inside, for it is visible in the pillars, ceiling beams, *shōji*, floors, *ranma*, lighting fixtures, and the like. But then, the lacquer applied over the wooden household things we touch with our hands—the food trays, buckets, and all manner of tableware—functions as a protection against water, abrasion, and staining of the surface.

Incidentally, the beauty of plain wood it is not just the result of the carpenter's technique. The process starts with the way you plant and grow the tree, that is, with the way you prune the branches and manage the annual rings. In Yoshino, Nara Prefecture, known for a tree now called the Yoshino cedar, they practice a foresting method called "dense planting" in which trees are planted twice as close together as in normal foresting. The resulting saplings constrain each other's development, thus growing more slowly. The trees respond by sending up long branches with dense foliage to get more sun. But because those branches are pruned early to avoid nodes in the trunk, leaves can only grow fully at the very top of the tree. Thus, these cedars continually stretch straight up in their quest for light. Furthermore, because of the way they are planted, each tree crowds the one next to it, preventing it from growing too large. This means the rings that mark one year's growth are thin and equally spaced. If the trees are raised in plentiful sunlight, the side facing the sun grows thicker. The annual rings follow suit, also becoming larger. In a word, dense planting is a technique to control the development of the rings by reducing a tree's exposure to the sun. If some trees cannot grow, due to the insufficient light, they are cut down without a second thought. Thus, the grain of cedars raised in this manner for one hundred, even two hundred years, is crafted, even artistic. Might this be called an art form, born of human intervention into nature's creative process?

The carpenter's techniques are what finally bring this plain wood into the realm of architecture, thus finishing its journey. The woodworker's plane applies the final touches to the lumber. The shavings deftly sliced away display a soft glossiness even finer than paper's. You can gain a glimpse of the spirit of the people who raised it in each tree.

080 The Ise Shrine

The shape of the *torii* at the Ise Shrine somehow puts you at ease. Just looking at them leaves one moved and enchanted. Torii have many shapes. Each follows a basic structure, but various aspects change from shrine to shrine—the warp of the top beam, the thickness of the pillars, or the korobi, i.e. the spread of the pillars as they approach the ground. The Ise Shrine's torii are magnificent edifices of unfinished wood, devoid of any ornamentation. The warp of their upper beam, the delicate width of their pillars, and the degree of their spread leave nothing to be desired. Perhaps due to the careful scrutiny that occurs during each dismantling and reconstruction—at intervals of twenty years according to the prescribed Ise Shrine schedule—inch by inch, these torii have evolved a shape that is etched deeply into the Japanese character.

Indeed, this can be said of all the Ise structures. The style is said to have originated from Polynesian architectural forms that crossed the Pacific. Yet through the uninterrupted process of being taken down and reconstructed every two decades over a thousand-and-some years, Ise architecture bit by bit changed its appearance, taking on a shape more and more intimately linked with Japanese sensibilities, pressing ever closer to what can only be called a purer Japan.

The prescribed schedule of the Ise Shrine means the reconstruction of every shrine building on an identical, prearranged neighboring site every twenty years. This is followed by ceremonies in which the gods and ritual objects are transferred to the new structures. The blueprints for both the structures and ritual articles are redrawn on each occasion. The head carpenter also changes. Reconstructing everything from scratch may seem unreasonable if one's goal is the preservation of tradition. But think again. The succession can be legitimate only if the art of reproducing those structures and articles is also handed down. The aim here is not merely to preserve the objects. Rather, tradition can be transmitted only when accompanied by the will to continue it and the requisite knowledge and skills, irrespective of material or immaterial concerns. Preservation is death. Reproduction, on the other hand, is the renewal of life. Thus, as with human existence itself, the mechanisms of progress necessarily function within the act of reproduction.

I expect the head carpenter strives for the ideal shape the moment he draws up new blueprints or runs his plane along a piece of lumber, slicing off a solitary wood shaving. But no matter how hard you strive, creating a perfectly identical object is impossible. Deviations inevitably occur. These differences gravitate towards their creator even as that creator strives towards his ideal. Progress occurs within this process. This repeated renewal, like the evolution of life itself, moves in a direction that conforms to the surrounding environment.

The Ise Shrine has been reborn sixty-two times; the last rotation was the sixty-second. If you count the time elapsed during delays, the process has lasted more than one thousand three hundred years. This renewal of existence is a kind of reincarnation. The reformed Shrine is the definition of *itoshiroshiki*. The glistening new life of a shrine standing next to the cast-off husk of itself is a perfect example of *shiroshi*.

081 Tatami

Tatami are not white per se. Yet these woven straw mats come across in the Japanese sensibility as white.

What distinguishes traditional Japanese housing from that of the West is materials—Japan uses wood and paper, the West stone and brick. But I believe the most striking difference is this: we take off our shoes to enter the house, then walk on tatami, the comfortable, hard-yet-soft flooring laid seamlessly across the floor. Even within Asia, no other region came to use tatami-like mats as flooring. The custom of removing one's shoes at the entranceway has recently been taken up in China, but historically that country resembled the West in that its people wore shoes over a rock or brick floor in their homes. People take off their shoes indoors in Korea as well. To counter the cold, Koreans developed the *ondol* floor heating system using a thick, multilayered form of paper as their flooring. Of course, wooden flooring is also common. But what makes Japanese housing unique is the tatami-laid *ma*—or "space."

The defining characteristic of homes in the Islamic world is their carpets, which are richly colored, covered in unique patterns, and laid over a hard earthen floor. The carpets are attractive, a dense weave of multicolored threads. Colors tend to encroach on each other when there are too many in a single design. Apparently, this blurring of primary colors is called "broken color" (muddied color) in Tibet. Surely, then, the Islamic world's multihued carpets are informed by something completely different. Thanks to their thickly woven fibers, a pleasant warm softness intervenes in the boundary between your body and the hard, cold floor. Furthermore, their intricate patterns paint the space with a range of feelings: a comfortable living space for the body, a holiness that fills one's inner space, and a fondness for the room.

Now to return to tatami. The bulk of the inner part of the tatami is called the *tatamidoko*—the core of the tatami—which is straw, the byproduct of rice harvesting. The bare straw is rough and coarse to the touch. This core is covered with a soft rush weave called the *tatami omote*—the face of the tatami. Add the cloth *tatamiberi*—the edging of the tatami—and the result is an ordered space both elegant and refreshing. There are many ways to weave a tatami, but in general its coarse surface evens out the floor's undulations, thus creating its characteristic flatness. Before the Muromachi period, tatami were placed so that you could see the borders of each one on the floor. By the end of the Muromachi period, however, the mats reached their perfected form of ma. Four and a half, six, eight, ten mats in increasing numbers were combined and used. As pure space, the rooms' ma exerts an influence on the actions of those who use it. It is thought to be the cause of our indoor demeanor—how we stand and sit, the way we open and close *shōji* and *fusama*, and so forth.

I long for a room where I can slide open the shōji on a moonlit night and gaze out at the garden from the veranda, inviting in the clear, serene light. The cool touch of the tatami's whiteness saturates my mind.

082 Light

The series of collapsible lanterns called Akari Light Sculptures, by the sculptor Isamu Noguchi, will shine through the ages. I feel a great sense of ease whenever I see one of those pieces. They are simple constructions of paper and bamboo, combinations of Mino *washi* and Gifu lanterns, but they shine in both Japanese and Western spaces, giving off a humble white light.

Isamu Noguchi was born to a strict Japanese father and a spirited American mother. Always curious, he observed the differing essences of Eastern and Western cultures from within his complicated upbringing. Indeed, I think he was the rare sort of person able to utilize his upbringing to gain an understanding of both sides. In his early work, Noguchi had a genius for form and would most likely have gone on to produce representational sculptures like those of Michelangelo or Auguste Rodin. He went to Paris, however, where he received instruction from Constantin Brâncuși, discovering in his own art an abstract style more suitable to exploring universals. Searching for fresh shapes and forms of expression Noguchi turned his gaze to Japan—to its gardens, paper, light, and the Anji stones of Sanuki Province.

Located in Takamatsu city, the Garden Art Gallery of Isamu Noguchi is like a lighthouse for our hearts. Inside the gallery grounds —surrounded by serene stone masonry—finished and unfinished works are scattered here and there at perfect intervals. Next to the grounds, standing side by side with just enough space between them, are an old private house (now a workshop) and a storehouse dedicated to Noguchi's reconstructed masterpiece, *Energy Void*. An expanse of sand covers part of the garden—one can almost hear a bamboo broom sweeping its surface. Visitors must stand and wait for a short time at the entrance, which is cordoned off by poles of green bamboo. Once these open, however, you step into a purified garden. I have visited this gallery more times than I can remember. The space, marked by groups of stones standing together, feels like a single sculpture. Each time I enter here I feel cleansed. Next to the main hall is a building that Noguchi used as a workshop, called the Isamu House. And there, placed in a corner where one can still sense the movements of this prolific sculptor, is a large Akari lantern.

The relationship between humans and fire is long and profound. The ability to manipulate fire made us who we are; it distinguishes us from animals. Human civilization began the moment we managed to carry tiny flames in our hands—hands that had been freed up by our bipedal gait. Firelight was the heart of our nights, for warmth and illumination. We lit modest fires for countless generations, until Thomas Edison's invention of the electric light. With our little fires we mined the night, opening its depth for our activities. The Japanese favored the faint light of a wax candle filtered through washi. We made framed and unframed paper lanterns, surfaces illuminated by a single point of candlelight, taking advantage of the way it penetrates and diffuses through paper. Beside these lamps, we quietly, secretly, pursued our nighttime goings-on.

Isamu Noguchi's Akari lanterns use electric light, but because it is filtered through unwrinkled washi its quality softens. The muted glow on their surfaces manifests an ancient sensibility that favors the subdued light of dusk.

083 Fans

The invention and dissemination of paper holds a unique place in the annals of human history. Paper was invented in Han dynasty China, which endured both before and after the B.C.E/C.E. line. At first, tattered hemp cloth was used for pulp, but that was later replaced by tree bark and bamboo. In either case—bark or bamboo—the ingredient was pulped, mixed with water, spread onto a paper-making screen, and dried in the sun. This process was transmitted to the Islamic world by prisoners taken during the war between the eighth century T'ang and Abbasid Caliphate dynasties. It spread to Anatolia as well as Northern and Western Africa, and then north to Southern Europe through Morocco. These white sheets fascinated people all over the world. Finally, they made their way to Northern Europe in the twelfth century, where they enabled the prosperous printing industry of fifteenth-century Germany.

At that time almost all papermaking—from China and the Islamic countries to Europe—used a method called that was called "accumulative": a screen is dipped into a tub filled with a fibrous mash and then lifted and gently shaken, a little at a time. If the fibers are not fine enough, the water passing through the screen will drip too quickly. To make the fibers workable, therefore, you must smash them until they are short. This results in paper with a thick, soft surface. Beautiful writing paper, in other words.

Concurrently, along a different historical trajectory, the paper-making process moved from China to the Korean peninsula, during the second to the fourth centuries. When it was transmitted to Japan in the seventh century, a new manufacturing process was devised called *nagashisuki* or "poured" paper. This process blended into the fibrous mash a highly viscous ingredient collected from the sunset hibiscus or panicle hydrangea plants. This slimy liquid enveloped the fibers, and the mixture was then poured repeatedly over a screen. This preserved the longer fibers, producing a tougher material with a densely entangled mesh. The thinner, stronger paper that resulted became viable not only as a material to write on, but also for structural purposes and the utensils of daily life. In Japan, paper was used to construct *shōji* and *fusama*, and made into various household items such as umbrellas, lanterns, and clothing. A floor heating system was devised on the colder Korea peninsula, where a robust paper called *ondol* was installed in layers.

The *uchiwa*, or fan, is common to both Japan and the Korean peninsula. A flexible, resilient piece of bamboo was cut and spread to form a delicate skeletal structure with the bottom part used as a handle. Thin paper was then pasted to both sides producing a tool that, like insect wings, displaced air. The paper was often reinforced with persimmon juice or glue. Nevertheless, had such thin, tough paper not existed, the uchiwa never would have been born. The folding *ōgi* fan has an elegance consistent with its craftsmanship, but the humble uchiwa works just as well to fan a fire or stir up a breeze. It may not reach the heights of book publishing or architecture, but I still find myself captivated by its clever construction. An uchiwa with nothing but white paper pasted over the bamboo skeleton is beautiful, somehow imparting its strength and tension when taken in the hand. Holding it, I feel as if I have been given a subtle nudge in the right direction.

084 Sample Dummy

A sample dummy is something you make when planning the design of a book. It is a sample volume where the pages are completely blank. One is produced each time a book is made, so I have gathered quite a few. At first glance they look featureless. But try picking one up—you will find it has a definite appeal. This is because the book is infused with traces of the bookbinding process.

Books are like informational sculptures. We would never put them on such a high pedestal if all they contained were facts or records, which tend to go in one ear and out the other. The advent of electronic books and websites means we can now compile information in an even more active way. Besides text and pictures, we can now store video, animation, and audio all in the same place. We can also share information freely. Since electronic information can be added to at any time, it never goes out of date; it can be easily launched and used for a long time. Thanks to this, the way we use our minds has also become more active. And yet, I think the value and significance of books is all the more obvious, precisely because of the constantly updated electronic information that now flows so freely. To print text or a picture with ink on paper is to have done something that cannot be undone. Thus, the content and data the pages contain must be correspondingly well researched and edited. The text must be aligned on the paper in an attractive way. Photos must be cropped and positioned in layouts that resonate beautifully with that text. Since the work is irreversible, each element has to be fine-tuned.

Even the book's paper must bear a relation to the content. Besides the accuracy of the text and its technical reproduction, one must also design the paper's feel, so that your fingertips can take pleasure in touching its natural fibers with every turn of the page. Furthermore, the breadth of the spine—that is, how thick the book should be, must also be considered. The possible hues of white the paper can take are near limitless—it can be the whitest of whites, or it can evoke the surface of snow or cotton. There are whites that suggest the gloss of silk or the warmth of an egg, the natural paleness of unbleached cloth or the faint tan of straw, florid whites that blush, grayish ones that hint at dull ash. Next, the paper's surface: glossy like glass or matte with a *hakuji* porcelain smoothness? A soft fabric-like texture, or a leathery, slippery surface that feels somehow humid? All the senses must be mobilized to select the paper that is the best complement for the book's contents.

These considerations extend beyond the pages of the main text. The binding that attaches the covers to the sewn signatures, the endpapers that lead from the cover to the main text, the decorated title page after the endpaper, then the jacket that envelops the binding, and the book's *obi*: a paper sash that, in Japan, is wrapped around the bottom of the finished book,

Take up a sample dummy in your hands and your fingertips will register the carefully selected whiteness—one chosen for this book and no other. Sweat will bead on your forehead. This experience is one of the many pleasures the era of bookmaking gave to us.

085 Decimal Point

How old was I when I first learned about decimals? I remember that it was quite an ordeal. It meant the world of prime numbers—which I had until then thought made up the entirety of numerals—were an egregiously oversimplified convenience. Suddenly standing between 5 and 6, for example, was an infinity of other possible numbers. I can vaguely recall the surprise verging on bewilderment I felt upon learning this. Then things like Pi or square roots—mathematical phenomena that however much you try can never be fully calculated, whose numbers continue into eternity after the decimal point—made me terribly uneasy, as if I were peering down into a bottomless pit. I felt a sense of relief, however, when these numbers were translated into abstract but clearly defined ideas or concepts, so that it was unnecessary to spell out their post-decimal infinity, as in π for Pi and $\sqrt{}$ for square roots. Differentials or integers are not just methods of calculation—they are a means of understanding the world. Set theory and probability theory, too, are pieces of analytical wisdom that help us to keep going—so to speak.

Design resembles mathematics. Design is about ascertaining the essence of things. It is an art that uses logic and rationality to shape our environments. Just as mathematic principles sit behind everything, everything that we have ever produced has been designed. The shape of bread, sugar cubes, spoons, chairs, light fixtures, guardrails, the tetrapods that line beaches—each is the product of a clearly thought-out plan. There is a reason manhole covers are round. If they were square or hexagonal, they would fall into the holes. There is a reason forks have four tines. Indeed, the book called *Why Did the Fork Come to Have Four Tines?* by Henry Petroski explores that question in great detail. Petroski's perspective, which considers engineering as "a series of failures," is richly suggestive. He traces the long process of trial and error that went into the fork's shape. The first fork, he explains, had two tines and was used to scoop food onto a knife that then carried the food to the mouth. But since the knife often cut the eater's mouth, the functions of scooping and carrying were gradually added to the fork, which in turn influenced the shape of the knife. In other words, Petroski explains, the knife and fork coevolved—they exerted an influence on each other. This really hit home for me. I assume experiments were also carried out on five- and eight-tined forks. Perhaps if we think hard enough, we might discover the mathematics of the fork in this process.

Toilet paper is round not just because it is easy to use, but because that makes it easy to manufacture. Attention to such details makes the world appear brand new. Everyday life becomes filled with an infinite wisdom. If the path to this realization is design, then it is similar to the surprise I felt upon learning the significance of the decimal point. This, too, is *shiroshi*.

086 Hōsun

I once constructed the following apparatus. A thin pipe stretches down from the ceiling to chest level. It has a nozzle on the end from which water slowly drips. The drips fall onto a thin plate about five centimeters in diameter. The plate has a pure white, hydrophobic coating. Because of this water-repellent surface, the drops of water form small spheres, circling the plate several times from the force of their descent before falling through a hole in the plate's center one by one. Below the plate, I set up a series of halved water pipes, each five millimeters wide and one meter long. The droplets run smoothly down the pipes, splashing from one to the next. Their course changes ever so slightly with each transfer.

The last pipe is set up at a steep angle. Arriving there, the droplets make a quick descent to fall onto a plate-like disk two meters in diameter. The disk has a shallow, cone-like surface set at a specific depth. The droplets falling from the final pipe slide along to circle the edge of the disk. They slowly move towards the disk's center in a spiraling motion, finally disappearing through a three-centimeter-square hole cut in the center of the disk. The droplets travel the circumference of the disk four, five times right up until the moment they disappear. The pipes and the disk are also treated with the matte white water-resistant coating. The droplets—and only the droplets—glitter in the light as they fall and rotate around the shallow disk. Once they plummet from the final pipe, they are difficult to see since they travel at such high speeds. As a result, the circling droplets appear to materialize one after the other on top of the disk. The effect is truly mysterious.

The droplets that fall through the square hole disappear into a round pond four meters in diameter, producing only the faintest ripples. I was commissioned to make this apparatus by the 21st Century Museum of Contemporary Art in Kanazawa city, as a part of an exhibition featuring objects designed to imitate the various aspects of the tea ceremony. The architect Kuma Kengo made a "tea room," the multimedia artist Iwai Toshio made a "garden," the product designer Fukasawa Naoto made a "meeting place," and I was charged with the "stone wash basin"—the *tsukubai*. My tsukubai, now separated from the other pieces, has been installed in a tranquil corner of a *ryokan* in Ishikawa Prefecture, where it joins a pond designed especially for the location by Takeyama Kiyoshi. The installation is in a lounge for visiting guests, a perfect place for it to reside.

I began constructing this piece in 2004 using hydrophobic technology, i.e. materials that perfectly repel moisture. I felt driven to produce a piece that was premised on controlling transparent droplets of water. It was the second work I produced, and I titled it *Hōsun*. This means one *sun*, or 3.03 centimeters, squared. In Zen, however, hōsun refers to the innermost center of a human being, the *kokoro*. This tiny inner place occupies the center of our chest.

The force of gravity works on the water droplets much as it holds the planets of our solar system in cone-like spirals. The spherical droplets express this force in their spiraling motion, glittering in the light until finally falling down into the hōsun.

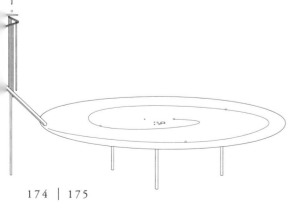

087 Embossing

"Embossing" is a term used in the manufacturing of paper. It refers to the process of pressing an engraving plate onto a sheet of paper, causing the text or icons to appear on the surface in delicate relief. This gives the paper an elegant appearance that will enhance the text or images that are then printed on it. Embossing is often used to increase the aesthetic value or emotional impact of a single sheet of paper—as with awards, written guarantees, and the like.

The photographer Kuyama Shiromasa, who attended the same Okayama high school as me, unexpectedly took a job in Tokyo more than twenty years after his graduation. The writer Harada Munenori, Kuyama, and I had been close, sometimes rascally friends since our high school days, so we started seeing each other in Tokyo right away. Kuyama and I once helped Harada with one of his novels—I designed the format based on Kuyama's photographs.

As a photographer Kuyama had a chivalrous spirit. It's not that he was heroic or fierce, just that he would fall in love with any object that caught his eye and capture it in photographs that had a certain affectionate clumsiness. His frankness, honesty, and deeply felt passion gave his pictures their style. He was always smiling. Once, during a photo shoot, he broke a bone and had to be hospitalized. When I went to visit him, however, he seemed to be having a great time, smiling ear to ear.

Despite having such vitality, Kuyama Shiromasa was diagnosed with terminal cancer of the gallbladder. This was just as he was beginning to photograph the regions struck by the 3.11 triple disaster a few months after the incident. The doctor told Kuyama that he might not live to see next year's *sakura*. Kuyama always desired to live life to the fullest so it was not an easy fate for him to accept. "I'm scared," he told me. "I don't want to die." But he was still smiling. I was heading home after visiting hours, and he saw me to the hospital elevator, his face still smiling as the doors closed. It was the last time I saw him.

Some time before, Kuyama had asked me to do him a favor before he died. It was to design an embossed image for a printed photograph. Another photographer had done this with photographic printing paper as one would with signatures or seals on writing paper, and Kuyama said he wanted to try it. His last act was to gather his loved ones together to have their pictures taken for this portrait on specially designed paper. So, on the chosen day, friends gathered at Kuyama Shiromasa's place. The occasion was filled with a calm intimacy. Coaxed by Kuyama's smiles, people's faces naturally relaxed. Apparently, his finger grew swollen and purple from pressing down on the shutter so many times, but I did not notice. I could only see that he seemed to be having a great time, a big smile on his face. He was his usual self.

A single tree laden with fruit, its branches drooping. This was the design I gave to Kuyama. I also gave him a press. He was delighted, embossing every piece of paper he could get his hands on. He gently embossed a monochrome portrait of me on one of the pictures he took at the portrait event.

088 Spitz

The spitz is a dog covered in long, white, fluffy hair. They are not seen much these days, but they were all the rage during Japan's economic miracle. Even I had a pet spitz named Chibi—which means "Small Fry"—around the time I graduated from high school. He was a male dog, very clever and gentle. His doghouse was at the end of the alley beside our house; it fit the passageway's width perfectly. Even though the doghouse had a peaked roof, Chibi liked to climb up there during the day to catch the rays of the sun. He would leap on the roof as soon as someone called "house!" We used the English word. It was my job to take him for a daily walk and so every evening at about five I took him out for about fifteen minutes. Thinking back on it now, I can see he didn't have much freedom. About the time I entered middle school my family moved to a place with a small yard, and there at last Chibi could run about a little. In his later years, we would untie his leash so he could roam on his own. He never strayed far and always returned about the same time. He was such a good dog that we barely had to lift a finger to care for him.

It was long ago, but I still remember in vivid detail the day I got Chibi. My father arrived home with a puppy in a cardboard box on the back of his bike. I can still hear the puppy's breathing as it slept beside the brazier in our house. Suddenly having a living creature join our family made my heart pound with excitement. The puppy grew in the blink of an eye. Soon it was impossible to keep him in the house, so my parents set up the doghouse outside. White dogs become dirty quickly, though. Sometimes we washed him in a tub filled with lukewarm water using a special shampoo designed for fur. That distinct, animal smell meant the dog was getting clean. When a spitz fresh from the bath shakes his body, water flies up everywhere causing a real commotion. A young spitz turns into a mass of white fluff after being washed.

Chibi was only allowed in the house at such times. Even then, though, my parents would go crazy when he ran around excitedly, scratching the *tatami* with his nails.

After a few years Chibi's health suddenly worsened. His white fur yellowed, and he lost all his energy. We realized how serious it was when he stopped eating. My father then pried open his mouth and forced him to drink milk though the dog cried out in protest. I thought this was extremely rough treatment, but it soon began to work wonders and, finally, the dog's energy returned. My father never seemed to me so strong and dependable as during this time.

In the new house, the garden become our meeting place. Chibi seemed content in his new domain. I spent a great deal of time with him in that garden filled with holly and olive plants, next to the veranda bathed in sunlight. As those tranquil days passed, he grew old. Then one day he again lost his vitality. We took him to the veterinarian who said it was a bad case of filariasis with no prospect of recovery. Grasping for any shred of hope, we asked the vet to do his best to treat him. The vet took him away in his car. Although utterly weak, Chibi suddenly jumped up and hung his front paws over the backrest as they left. He seemed to be leaning in our direction, his eyes fixed on us. The car grew smaller as it drove away. Chibi did not recover. Even now my heart aches when I see a white spitz. I wish we had cared for Chibi at home in his final moments.

089　The Moon

I think I only became truly aware of the moon during the Apollo 11 moon landing. As children we first get to know the sun and the moon—the most beloved celestial phenomena—through fairy-tales and fables, so I was certainly aware of the moon in that way. Yet, before I was old enough to gaze up at it with my beloved, before I could reimagine it through the rhetorical flourishes of a *tanka* or *haiku*, humanity had already reached its surface.

It was an early July morning in 1969. I was in elementary school. My father, mother, and I were sprawled out on the futon, our eyes glued to a long-legged TV set. We could see the moon landing vessel descending towards the moon's surface projected on the curved screen of the CRT, our black-and-white TV set. I missed the definitive moment when Captain Armstrong stepped down. Watching a televised rerun of the event, though, I felt I had been transported there. The footprints are burned onto my retinas. They remember the ash-like quality of our modest moon's surface as a series of grays.

The more you think about the relationship between the sun, the moon, and the earth, the more clearly it encapsulates the mysteries of the universe. Witness, for example, the unusual brightness of a supermoon —a periodically occurring phenomenon in which the moon appears larger than usual—and you cannot help but be reminded of the fact that we exist in the vacuum of space. The sun is so bright it cannot be looked at directly. What a bizarre fact of life! If looking at the sun had been necessary for survival, then our eyes would have evolved that ability. If it is too bright to look at, that must mean we had no need to do so. But not the moon—we can see it so clearly that even the patterns on its surface are visible. So clearly that we all see a rabbit pounding *mochi*. Perhaps this means there is something we need to discern in its white, faint glow.

There is an open-air platform called the *tsukimidai*—literally, moon-viewing pedestal—attached to the Old Shoin study in the Katsura Imperial Villa. I had assumed this bamboo-built, stage-like space was set up as a spot to view the moon. Now I was struck, however, by a different theory—that it may have been designed to reflect moonlight. Somehow this was easier to imagine. The Villa was built in an era when nights were very dark, lit only by wax candles and pine torches. In such darkness, the full moon would have been so bright that its intense light pouring onto the surface of the bamboo-made balcony would have been wonderful. Imagine the elegance of gazing out into that brightness through wide-open *shōji*—could there be a better way to enjoy nature? I sigh just thinking about such aesthetic mastery. You would feel the presence of an entire culture taking delight in bright moonlight and the air of a clear autumn night.

A whole family wrapped in quilts watching the moon landing scene on a black-and-white television is several centuries removed from this tsukimidai. The next landmark journey will probably be to Mars. Unlike the moon, however, Mars is distant from the earth. Thus, a trip to the planet would have to be timed to take place when it is closest to us, which happens about once every two years. No getting around that travel time, though—a full year, one way.

090 Rhythm

There is a phrase in Japanese that means "to catch off guard"—a literal translation would be "to strike an opening." In martial arts, that involves seizing the advantage when your opponent's rhythm falters, allowing you an opportunity. By recognizing a lapse in his defense, you can score a point.

The rhythms of the universe are in everything—in the axis rotations and orbital revolutions of planets around a star; in the push and pull of proximity and estrangement between moon and earth and the corresponding ebb and flow of the tides; in the changing seasons; in the alternation of night and day; in sleeping and wakefulness; in our breathing and the beat of our hearts; in blinking and yawning; in an RNA molecule reading the base sequence of DNA deep within our bodies.... I believe all these and more are somehow interconnected.

The "Kecak" is an Indonesian seated ritual in which a large group of people rock and shake their bodies while calling out in chorus. Filled with praise for life, and sensually linked to the rhythms of existence, the chant grabs us—and it doesn't let go. The chorus is broken into sections: *"Chak, chak, chak, kecak, kecak, kecak, kecak...."* is sung with gusto and punctuated with calls of *"Haa, haa, haa, shiriri, haa, haa, haa, shiriri."* This establishes the base rhythm of the dance. It struck me that *haa* was the "on" beat and *shiriri* the "off." That is, after three down-beats, the fourth beat is the shiriri up-beat. In that rhythm, the singers exerted themselves on the first three beats and rested on the fourth. My teacher, Mukai Shūtarō, once said form is a gesture that responds to the living things of the universe. Perhaps the reason I was so touched watching the flow and convergence of those bodies is that the dancers were so deeply connected with the rhythms of the universe.

The compositional rules of Western music, whose foundation was laid by Bach, are so noble and subtle you are left to wonder whether humans are actually responsible for their ordered being. The Kecak too is a type of systematically expressed gesture that responds to the human universe—i.e. existence.

Japanese music approaches things differently. It seeks to disrupt the idea of rhythm as a source of ease that calms the body. Western jazz, too, performs a kind of rhythmic acrobatics by meandering all over the place. Unlike Japanese music, however, it keeps the overall rhythm perfectly in time. Contrastingly, Japanese music insists on deviations; that is, it aims to catch its listener off-guard.

A musician who plays the *tsuzumi*—a type of hand drum—plays a game of catch-me-if-you-can with the expected downbeats. When we listen to music, a beat is established, and our senses can predict when the next sound should occur, as precisely as machine-gun fire. The tsuzumi player, however, acts like a ninja, avoiding the rhythmically arriving projectiles as they pass through the arena that is music. The same with the *shakuhachi*—an end-blown bamboo flute. The moment your ears have eased comfortably into the musical pulse, the *hyoo* of the flute strikes where you don't expect it. Our perpetually-on-guard sense of "Here it comes! Here it comes!" is deftly turned aside. The music is played like a veteran boxer who skillfully bobs and weaves around punches.

Design, I have often felt, resembles *kendō*, which I grew up practicing. I believe the art of engaging people's feelings lies in the secrets of rhythmic deviation, that is, in openings and margins.

091 Emptiness

"Intricacy" has shaped the world. This is because human history has been carved out by rulers. Apart from overwhelming power, rulers had to aquire prestige, something that would strike fear in the hearts of the populace and cause them to obey. This required not only military might, but also symbolic representations of authority. It is here we see the emergence of dense and intricate patterns. Elaborate ornamentations —the joining of high technical skill and abundant labor—demonstrated a ruler's miraculous achievements and made people shudder with awe. Thus, complicated designs were added to buildings, fixtures, and ritual vases. The dragon crests of China were an intricate tangle of coils. Arabesque designs eventually came to cover the entire surface of an object. The geometric arabesque of the Islamic world, like the baroque and rococo styles of the absolute rulers of Europe, were symbols of expansive power. In short, the dense patterns that filled the world were the masks of power. They were forms of intimidation and deterred rebellion as well as enemy attacks.

The world had to wait for the arrival of a mature industrial society to escape this intricacy, for only then could it begin exploring the shortest distance between material, function, and form—in other words, rationality, based on simplicity. In this modern society, a common person can play a leading role.

Japan is an island country situated at the eastern tip of the Eurasian continent. But if you rotate the standard map a quarter turn to the right, the Japanese archipelago appears near the bottom. If you liken this shape to a *pachinko* machine, the archipelago forms the tray beneath the Asian continent where the small metal pachinko balls collect. I find this image, contained in *An All-New Way to Read the World Map* by Takano Hajime, to be a truly revelatory observation. A ball is dropped somewhere around Rome and bounces about the various Eurasian countries before settling in Japan. Our country was a melting pot of influences received from cultures all over the globe. As the world overflowed with elaborate ornamentation, Japanese culture naturally became filled with a dazzling beauty.

The situation changed with the outbreak of the Ōnin War (1467–1477) in Kyoto. Much of Japan's tangible culture was lost during the decade-long conflict. Ashikaga Yoshimasa, the retired *shōgun* at that time, had distanced himself from politics, preferring to refine his already keen aesthetic sense. The world-renowned Ginkaku-ji in the Higashiyama region of Kyoto, officially named Jishō-ji, began as Yoshimasa's retirement villa. Yoshimasa had taken the opportunity to build it after handing over the shōgunate to his son. The aftermath of the Ōnin war's destruction was surely dreadful for the Japanese people of the time. The culture that grew around Yoshimasa after his retirement, however, was unlike that of the prewar period. It had an elegant simplicity that was the antithesis of showiness and luxury. Plainness and brevity in design allows people to invest their feelings far more freely than elaborate, delicate carvings and ornamentation. A unique aesthetic sense grounded in absolute "emptiness" emerged in the *shoin* and tea rooms, the *tokonoma* alcoves and flower arrangement spaces, the rock and plant gardens of Ginkaku-ji.

The character for emptiness in Japanese—read as *kara*—can also be read as *utsu*. In the latter case, the character refers to a state of hollowness, where there is nothing but empty space inside an object. Silence stirs up the imagination far better than aesthetic prolixity. A hollow holds the possibility of being filled. At a crossroads of its history, Japan took the pathway toward "simplicity," led by a philosophy that found abundance in emptiness.

092 Squares

We humans like to design square environments for ourselves. We divide up the organic earth with rectangular grids of roads. We mill trees into square shapes to build countless square structures. Even today, we construct rectangular buildings with square doorways, and go up and down in square elevators. We turn at square corners in hallways and open rectangular doors to see square rooms with square furniture and square windows. Thus, the landscapes framed in the windows are also square. The tables, cabinets, and televisions, even the remotes that control the televisions, are also square. We tap on rectangular keyboards for square computers sitting on square desks. We write out text on rectangular paper. The envelopes we slip that writing paper into are rectangular and the stamps we affix to them are square. Only the postmarks pressed onto the envelopes are sometimes round.

Why have we divided our environments into so many squares and rectangles? Honey bees seem to prefer hexagons. The spiders that spin their noble webs affirm this preference. Take a quick survey of nature and you will find that squares appear almost nowhere. One would expect nature to contain at least some mathematical expressions of "four." A square, however, is an unstable shape and thus materializes only infrequently. A square spider web, for example, would be flimsy indeed. I have seen a mineral crystallization of a perfect cube, so squares do appear sometimes. But they are the rare exceptions. It is not as if three-legged chairs and tables are unsteady. Yet, we have always obstinately chosen squares and four legs.

Perhaps this relates to the way we stand and sit upright, or to the fact that we have a right and left eye, and bilateral limbs. Attuned to the vertical pull of gravity, our senses must always be engaged, albeit unconsciously. The countervailing pull is the horizontal. Perhaps our hands, which so easily shape straight lines and right angles, determine our preference for squares. Other organic shapes, like the banana leaf, are split into two sides with a straight line separating them. If you make yet another fold over this first line of symmetry, you will have right angles. Extend that again and you have a square. The length and width of paper has a ratio of 1:√2. Sheets are configured so that this ratio will stay the same no matter how many times you fold it, vertically or horizontally. It appears that as our bodies encountered the world, we found squares to be our basic formula—i.e. the principle that we could familiarize ourselves with most easily. Thus, even the most cutting-edge computers and portable terminals take on this classic form.

Among right-angled shapes, the square has a special place. It feels like a foundational principle that humans stumbled upon while manipulating the natural world. The perfect circle may be the same. But while the circle is immanent in both the universe and humanity, the square somehow epitomizes the human intellect. Of course, this is just my opinion. And since we are speaking of that which is subjective, I think squares are white. Red squares, black squares—all of them are white.

093 Gardens

The gardens of the Hōjō, the "abbot's chamber" at the Tōfuku temple, were designed by Shigemori Mirei, master gardener and garden historian. The north garden has a checkered pattern formed by the alternating placement of square stones and lushly growing moss. The moss pushes upward as if trying to pour out onto the stones, while the systematic rows of stones appear to oppose the overflowing excess of life by imparting a clear order. The geometric pattern of the sunken stones seemingly holding back the moss's force and vigor as it attempts to swell upward creates a fascinating contrast between natural forms.

I always think of Isamu Noguchi's *Water Stone* sculpture when I see this garden. The top of the sculpture is a polished flat surface with a circular hole drilled in the center. Water slowly wells up from the bottom of this round hole. The rising water reaches a point of maximum surface tension, and if you look closely you can see it ooze out in all directions under the force of its flow as it begins spilling over. It wets the whole stone. Then the water begins to rise again. Just as the title implies, it is a stone wrapped in an unending flow of tranquil water.

Both works, the garden and the installation, are apparatuses that evoke the overabundance of life and its simultaneous restriction. Life overflows; it wells upward. That fact is brought home to a viewer by the sight of luxuriant moss surrounding square stones or water swelling out of a stone.

It goes without saying that a garden is planned and managed, but it is also a product of time and nature. In other words, the highlight of a garden is that it is the site of an ongoing exchange between artifice and nature. Erudite commentaries on its meaning—like the notion that a series of rocks symbolizes the cosmic Buddhist mountain Mt. Sumeru, or that stripes raked in sand represent the world's oceans—just seem to get in the way. How will those that come after you experience a garden filled with conspicuous displays of human artifice—in the placement of stones, the arranging of trees or moss, the laying down of white sand? Will they tolerate a garden that indulges in showy originality, a torrent, one might say, of mistakes? Will they come to love it? Protect it and pass it on to the next generation? Cultivate it? Will the attention that refines the garden—the cleaning and grooming, the thoughts and feelings accumulated in the process—touch the hearts of its viewers?

A garden is a place where artifice and nature collide, where order and chaos are bitter opponents. Nature possesses a generative and also a degenerative power. The lush growth of plants is an outpouring of life that artifice strives to negate. You could say that a garden's order is perpetually undermined by changing nature. Thus, people push against this gradual change, always tidying and pruning, striving to preserve the garden's intrinsic value.

Such an approach relies on artificiality while at the same time patiently accepting the excesses of nature. An outstanding garden seduces people to work on it over time. It opposes chaos as it attempts to generate meaning and significance by marshaling a wealth of information. In this book, I have called this *shiroshi*.

It was the summer of 1997, and I was visiting the designer Yagi Tamotsu, who was at that time based in San Francisco. I had no particular errand in mind. I was just dropping in for a visit since I happened to be staying close by. This was my first meeting with Yagi. Right off the bat, he pulled out an architecture magazine and showed me two buildings. Each had been designed by a Swiss architect. The first was a recently completed winery in Napa Valley by Herzog & de Meuron Basel. The second was a hot springs hotel in a village called Vals nestled in the Swiss Alps by Peter Zumthor. Showing each other objects of interest is a pleasant way for creators to introduce themselves, a form of etiquette perhaps. Moreover, I have a weakness for architecture. In fact, when I first started studying design and became more familiar with it, I nearly decided to re-take my entrance exam to enter the architecture department instead. Yagi Tamotsu had seemingly got wind of this. I felt a shock when he showed me these two buildings, as if something had zapped my heart.

The winery was a curious structure. Sturdy wire netting had been stretched over frames to form box-like containers crammed full of heavy, unworked white stones. Apparently, in Switzerland such stones are used instead of sandbags to protect against landslides. The cubes of stone-filled wire mesh formed a long, narrow, rectangular construction, which was enshrined in the middle of the vineyard as a conspicuous geometrical figure. Since there were small gaps between the stones, air and light passed through the cubes. The photographs of diffused light pouring into the building's interior overwhelmed me.

The hotel was a handsome building whose walls were laminated with thinly sliced stones taken from the immediate area. There is not a single cornered tub in the bathhouse. The hotel lobby looks like an underwater labyrinth, with pathways disappearing around corners.

It also connects to a massive outdoor pool. There are two pipes in the pool—reminiscent of the huge plumbing pipes you might find in a factory—that emerge from the steam. Hot water gushes from their downturned spouts.

Still taken aback by Yagi Tamotsu's preemptive architectural strike, I headed out towards Napa Valley to visit the winery after our visit ended. Not too long after that, I sought out Peter Zumthor's building in the snowy Swiss Alps. My heart was once again swept away by the sight of a rectangular building set against the snow-covered, natural topography.

Architecture is like gardening. But it is shaped even more by human will. Architecture, which in ancient times was sacred because it symbolized nature, has come to seem even more radiant as a symbol of reason. The buildings of Le Corbusier and Ludwig Mies van der Rohe feel particularly white, but not because they were painted that way. Rather, they shimmer as man-made figures confronting nature. Artifice is not destruction. The spectacle of human hands struggling against nature occasionally yields a brilliant light.

095 The Drawn White Sword

The Japanese *katana* differs from the straight, double-edged swords found in the west. The blade has a subtle curve, with an edge, or ridge, at top and bottom. An observer can tell how well the sword is made by the tip and the degree to which what is called the ridgeline bulges outward. It is the object most commonly designated as a national treasure. The shape of the katana was painstakingly arrived at in the pursuit of a clearly understood function. Perhaps this explains why it surpasses mere utility to evoke a sense of beauty. Yet no one can look at it without thinking of death. Not a natural death ending a long life either, but one that abruptly severs all ties with life.

Living organisms take a variety of forms, appropriating the lives of others where necessary so that they themselves may go on living. But we are unique among our fellow creatures in that we developed a tool—an edged tool—that extends our ability to kill and maim.

The proficiency with which one infringes on others' lives is considered an art, one of the "military arts." The development of the sword also caused our bloodlust to grow. Since the era of stone implements, we have altered our environment with every tool we have invented. New tools produced new desires, which in turn required more tools. Stone tools were soon replaced by bronze, and then by iron. The katana was created at a time of bitter civil strife and represents that era's view of life and death. The attempt to take life from another is a bargain whereby one puts up one's own life in possible exchange. In such a worldview, "the art of the blade" cuts both ways.

The katana in today's museums exert a bewitching and dangerous attraction, not just because of their deadly potential, but because of their unique sacredness as tools made to take life. Perhaps we also sense in them the artistry of their creators.

I have some experience with *kendō*, but the act of using a real sword in hand-to-hand conflict is now divorced from this martial art. All the madness of slaughter has been expunged. Kendō is a refined art capable of producing a disciplined fighting spirit. The bamboo katana was first introduced during the Edo period, a time of peace. Thus, kendō differs from battle in that one need not risk one's life. Indeed, my hair stood on end the first time I held a real katana. Its razor edge made it horrible to look at. Tales of master swordfighters go hand in hand with fantasies of cutting down your enemies, dispatching them one after another with your superior swordplay. The actual sensation of drawing your katana from its scabbard to face an opponent, however, is unimaginable. However exceptional the katana you wield, it can't be easy advancing on an armor-clad adversary determined to cut you down with a single stroke. I imagine drawing a sword is impossible unless you first fully resign yourself to death.

Seppuku, a ritual suicide accomplished by slitting open one's stomach, was done with a dagger. The ritual was performed as follows: dress in white clothing and sit. Wrap the dagger's blade in white paper. Hold the blade by gripping the paper. Carry out the deed.

096 Hand-to-Hand Combat

The landing at Normandy in World War II is realistically depicted in the opening scenes of the film *Saving Private Ryan*. A flotilla of landing craft that seems to cover the entire ocean advances towards the beach. Each boat, however, sits squarely in the sights of the Nazi machine guns placed in the fortifications built along the coastline. The moment the boats reach the shoreline, their doors open, and a barrage of bullets pours down from above. What an absurd way to fight a war! To seize victory by calculating the number of enemy bullets and then adding just enough soldiers to exceed that number is a cruel and inhuman tactic. Must war really be fought this way?

Look at the way the Battle of 203 Meter Hill was fought in the Russo-Japanese War, or how the landing was organized at Normandy. Consider the emotional impact. The strategy started with the assumption that many soldiers would die, and that the opponent would be overpowered by the stamina of those who survived. What possesses the soldiers to agree to this self-sacrificial warmongering? Is it the product of an aberrant mentality in which mind and body become a welter of strife and slaughter, one drop in a wave of rage? Is it possible for any mind to accept that a life is worth nothing more than a single bullet?

Bows, spears, and swords were abandoned as weapons because they conflicted with the new desires generated by the introduction of guns. The gun evolved into machine guns and even more destructive artillery, and then into tanks and battleships. Now we are faced with the abomination of nuclear warheads. Missiles launched from an aircraft or submarine can be precisely controlled to guarantee they hit their targets. The shape of desire changes with the evolution of weapons.

The idea of justice is always invoked to defend the drive for hegemony. I do not intend to claim here that nothing is more important than a single human life. Humanity does in actual fact occasionally sacrifice individual lives for causes it believes to be important. Nevertheless, if humanity is to stand on the side of life, to secure the continuation and prosperity of our species, then we have undeniably expanded the art of war to a foolish degree.

The futility of warfare and the transience of a soldier's life were well understood in the era of hand-to-hand combat—in Japanese, literally "white soldier combat"—when the tool that warriors fought with, the *katana*, was in full sight. The minute we unsheathed the double-edged sword that is science, our new desire drove us towards an idiocy that could destroy the world many times over. The fault does not lie with humanity in general. Rather, the battle is fought inside the mind of each person in a unit mobilized for war.

Evolutionary theorists sometimes posit plants as a more sophisticated life form than humans. It goes without saying that the "thinking reed"—us, in Pascal's phrase—looks down on the other, real reeds, but plants are never of two minds when it comes to securing their future generations. When I think of the foolishness of the military mind, I get the nagging sense that humans lag far behind plants on the intelligence front.

When set against the awesome forces of nature, man-made objects come to appear modest. The universe is inherently full of potential. The possibilities are infinite. There may well be worlds beyond imagining just waiting to be discovered. We do not know where we will end. We press bravely on, fumbling through the environment into which we have been born.

We have unflaggingly sought to discover truths about nature and the history of our planet, and finally arrived at some understanding. Though we have made progress in biology and the other sciences, the meaning of existence continues to evade us. We may never know it.

Ever since the appearance of single-celled organisms, life has taken on an ever-greater diversity, so that now an innumerable variety swarm about the surface. Biologists tell us that there is no pyramid-like hierarchy in the world of living things. Rather, everything is in mutual dependence on everything else. The single-celled organisms that exist today are direct descendants of the first ones. Humans, too, are nothing more than a single dot on an evolutionary arc. Thus, we cannot say which is more highly evolved, single-celled organisms or human beings. This is because we developed our current shape over a great stretch of time. We have not surpassed fish, nor are we smarter than plants. Pascal may object, but do not common reeds think? They simply do not think like humans. And if we are speaking from the point of view of the continuation of the species, then plant-like thought may be more sophisticated than our own.

We are impatient creatures, constantly on the move to gather food. Individual cells do not make their own decisions. Instead, they are made to perform by the brain, which developed to become the command post of our activity. In our system, the limbs and muscles execute according to the brain's instruction. Furthermore, since our invention of the concept "I," our concern for life tends to be limited to a single generation. By contrast, we are told each plant cell makes its own decisions, all directed towards the continuation and prosperity of an existence that extends over several generations

When you step through a thriving equatorial rainforest or glide through the sea over a bustling coral reef, you feel life's determination and tenacity. You observe how it forms cooperative networks with the aim of preserving itself. Humanity surely conceived of "I" as an efficient means to protect a single generation. By doing so, however, we may have limited our ability to consider future generations, severing ties between the realms of life and death. As a result, we have come to fear dying more than we should.

"I" is a drifting illusion that has lost touch with the wilds where greens and browns contend with each other. Clutching "I," humanity hovers alone in stark whiteness, living life one generation at a time.

098 Cleaning

What makes us preserve the environment built by those before us? Our enduring will to live. Leave things unattended and they immediately begin to return to their natural state of equilibrium. An abandoned house quickly collects dust, which becomes a hotbed for microbial growth. Pillars and beams slowly decay as rain quietly infiltrates and microbes multiply. Grass sprouts from sodden tatami. After several decades, the whole house, even its frame, will have rusted away, having supported an ecosystem of nonhuman, codependent living creatures.

Ancient structures made of stone are sometimes found in dense forests. Apparently they escape annihilation because they are constructed out of minerals less susceptible to erosion. If they had been made from materials easily destroyed or displaced by the filaments of plants and trees, they would have disappeared without a trace. We instinctively understand this risk. Thus, we clean, staving off the gathering of dust and dirt. At bottom we strive to preserve our present condition.

Japanese begin their housecleaning with a thorough dusting. We open windows to ensure good ventilation before we start. When dust rises, it inevitably recollects in a new place. Some drifts out the window, some falls to the floor. A good flow of air sends more outdoors, but the rest migrates to the floor. Thus, we whisk the fallen dust into a dustpan with a broom, or else sweep it outside. Then we take a cloth and firmly but carefully wipe shelves and floor using fabric and moisture to remove the remaining dust.

It takes a great deal of time and effort to preserve the cleanliness of a white ceramic toilet and the room where it sits. A clean washroom, however, is symbolic; it expresses how dedicated you are to a sense of purity in your everyday life. A clean washroom tells me its owner is a careful person, who possesses a healthy ambition. Is it not the case that a vase of a flowers is displayed, not just for a guest, but to signify the resident's internal conversation about the state of his space?

I once thought vaguely that cleaning indicated something else, namely our guilt about the fact that, as living creatures, we must pollute to live. Of course, this is one way to look at it. But now I am convinced that how we look after our homes and environments resonates with our lives. They are manifestations of our active, animated will. Cleaning manifests our unspoken determination to survive. We feel moved when noticing old structures and gardens being skillfully cared for because it proves that the will of those who first inhabited these places continues on. Even if an ancient site returns to the chaos of nature, it still possesses an *itoshiroshiki* form. Indeed, that very preservation of a will is synonymous with what it means to live.

099　Revision

We constantly revise our environment. To live is to construct. Design carries out this work of continual renewal and revision, yet its eyes are always fixed on the shape that an ideal environment might take.

We all know design is about shaping, that is, about color, form, and texture, and about motion, rhythm, and balance. This is true of course. But designers do more than just manufacture things with different colors and shapes. Rather, our aim is to offer a fresh outlook on whatever we produce by utilizing and bringing out these qualities. Just as important as shaping an object, we strive to heighten the "tautness" of the relationship between people and their environments.

When we hear the word *communicate*, for example, we tend to think it means "to make someone understand." To understand, however, is more than being able to explain, or give the definition of something. Rather, experiencing something you thought you knew in a fresh way—as though you had never come across it before—is more integral to what it means to truly comprehend an object. Design triggers the excitement that accompanies a deeper experience of the world. It increases those moments when we feel intense interest in things out there and are moved to approach them more closely.

I have referred to paper's whiteness. One always risks making a mistake when writing on a pure white, easily dirtied or damaged sheet. But we overcome this danger, again and again, when we inscribe something on this whiteness. If paper is a medium that inspires creativity, then record-taking and the imparting of information are secondary to its nature. Its primary purpose, therefore, is to push us to create, even in the face of failure. Paper, with its whiteness and fragile tautness, is in this sense a truly outstanding medium.

Like design, architecture also participates in environmental revision and renewal. This is true across styles, from Roman to Tokyo

Metabolist. Architects deepen their understanding of urban living through the process we call planning, identifying the purpose each building should have. They assess space and structure, consider light, and plot shadow. They test materials, examine construction methods, and transform ideas into reality. What shakes a city awake and sets it in motion? The surging hopes and desires of its people. Is our environment, however slowly, finally approaching an ideal through these continual revisions?

I believe there is a place in the center of my being where the waves I receive from the universe and the waves that I send out from the universe within me struggle against each other. I would call this place a beach—in Japanese, 波打ち際, or "a border pounded by waves." It is the whiteness of that beach that led me to become a designer. The things I have designed seem trivial—after all, a hundred years go by in the blink of an eye. But the force that attempts the endless journey towards whiteness is surely rooted within "me." This "me" is not some isolated fragment of a static whole. On the contrary, it may well be that my existence is part of an unbroken chain stretching into antiquity.

100 One Hundred

I liked the work of Austrian painter Friedensreich Hundertwasser when I was in high school. Painting in a strange but interesting style, Hundertwasser created brightly colored dream worlds using tree-ring-like, circular formations that proliferated across the canvas. However, it's not his work I'd like to discuss here, but his name. In German, *hundert* means "one hundred" and *wasser* means "water." Thus, his name literally means "hundred-water." An abstract image, to be sure, but in high school I felt a name like "one hundred waters" was truly romantic.

"One hundred" denotes a specific number, of course, but can also often mean "a great deal of something." It makes me imagine a dense growth, like a colony of white mushrooms growing in a thick forest or the crowded houses on the island of Mykonos. I can also imagine something gushing from the ground like a spring. Thus, the name "hundred-water" is deeply planted in my mind, an imagined fountainhead from which life surges forth.

Add a 1 (一) to the character for white (白) and you get the character for one hundred (百). *Kanji* are mysterious things. In this way, one hundred feels like white with one more degree of whiteness added to it. Ordinary oxygen (O_2) is made up of two oxygen atoms. But if you stick three oxygen atoms together, you are left with ozone (O_3). So then, what if we think of white as having ninety-nine atoms, so that adding one more white atom will give us "one hundred"? White is already white enough. Push it that tiny bit further, however, and you will be rewarded with an overabundance of whiteness, even more opaque and dense. That is the whiteness of "one hundred."

Of course, I did not give this book the title *100 Whites* to refer to such a white whiteness. As I wrote in my book *White*, there is no such thing as white—rather, it is a sensibility we experience. That is, in *White* I offered speculations centered around whiteness as an idea. This book, by contrast, attempts to capture various aspects of whiteness in concrete phenomena.

Furthermore, I felt *100 Whites* matched the idea of an unbroken series of entries about whiteness. It felt as if the contours of all the things I had experienced as white—things stashed away in the drawers of my memory—would rise through the mist one by one, allowing me to pick them out.

I had thought that "whiteness" meant something vividly brought into relief out of a chaotic, indistinct background. As I continued writing, though, I realized that I was actually trying to reach for the origin of life itself. Whether viewed macroscopically or microscopically, it was the source of power, an eternally spinning balance wheel of renewal.

At first I thought I would try to write the book without using the adjective "white" a single time. But that felt too unnatural. In the end, I decided to go with my instincts and use "white" to describe, somewhat forcibly, phenomena that carry a sense of renewal or awakening. In this final entry, for example, I have used "white" to my heart's content.

In any case, I drew the full circle of whiteness with the almost too white exuberance that is "one hundred."

Afterword or A Harmony of Senses

I am at the equator, on one of the Galápagos Islands, making the final edits to the *100 Whites* manuscript. The Galápagos are reddish-brown volcanic islands. They surfaced in the ocean five million years ago following the eruption of a submarine volcano and were further shaped by tectonic plate movements and repeated volcanic eruptions. It is thought that the giant tortoises arrived three million years ago, while the iguanas drifted ashore one and a half million years ago, perhaps arriving on a piece of driftwood. These animals managed to adapt to the conditions here and proceeded to evolve. The islands' natural features present a simple environment. Furthermore, without any human presence, the natural environment kept its purity. And yet if we were to reach out our hands to touch it, all could vanish in an instant. The islands are therefore filled with a fragile "tautness"—a perfect place for proofreading a manuscript about whiteness. I thought I had put all I had into each entry, but rereading them here, isolated from the world, I find nothing but problems. Thus, though I am feeling something resembling frustration, I will make my edits and soldier on.

Writing this book was a smooth process, carried out over the course of two years. I could probably do another hundred if asked, but anything beyond this point would only lead to redundancies. One hundred is just the right amount. A thousand would come to feel unmanageable, and if I shot for ten thousand, I'd probably abandon the project. At incredibly large numbers like one hundred million or one trillion, the image I was trying to capture would lose focus. If it was one hundred, though, I could manage. Picture one hundred *onigiri* or *daifukumochi*, or light one hundred wax candles, and you will be hit with a sense of abundance. Visit the same temple or shrine one hundred times to pray and something might just happen. Eating a hundred bowls of *soba* seems possible if someone will serve it to you.

The human life span is gradually approaching one hundred years—indeed, it is no longer unusual for people to live beyond even that great age. On the other hand, the shortest distance in a track-and-field event is one hundred meters. I don't know how they decided that, but that distance now determines the world's fastest runner. In any case, I have somehow managed to complete my own "one hundred."

Postscript

I could not have published these essays without a place to publish them. My will simply isn't strong enough to sit down and write one hundred entries without some kind of deadline. I would therefore like to offer my sincerest thanks to Yomiuri Online for offering me space to take on this experiment. It must have been difficult to configure a website to accommodate vertical script, but the weekly installments provided a wonderful sense of motivation for me. I would also like to express my gratitude to the immensely talented photographer Ueda Yoshihiko whose photographs appeared alongside the original serialization of this book. Working with Ueda in the Galápagos Islands was an undeserved honor. I could say much more, but as this book is centered around the essays, I would like to instead convey here my respect and appreciation.

I would also like to express my heartfelt gratitude to Hashizume Fumika of Chūōkōron-Shinsha, who was the first to read the essays during the original serialization. I thank her for her thoughtful comments and suggestions, and for her continued encouragement. Her attentiveness as my working partner was like a lighthouse in the haze of my everyday life.

I would also like to thank Nippon Design Center as well as all the staff at the Hara Design Institute who lent their support to my daily work as a designer, which formed the conceptual background for this manuscript. It is because you have enabled me to be single-minded about my work that I was able to extend my activity to the designing of words. I would also like to express my appreciation to Nishi Tomoko who proofread the manuscript and offered painstaking assistance in the design of this book.

Finally, I would like to take the opportunity to express my gratitude to my wife who is always there to calmly lead me back to my senses after I have, once again, drifted away into the lofty world of aesthetics.

Kenya Hara

Born in 1958, Kenya Hara is a graphic designer and professor at the Musashino Art University. Alongside "things," Hara's aim is to construct "circumstances" and "conditions."

His exhibitions *RE-DESIGN*, *HAPTIC*, and *SENSEWARE* have been shown all over the world, each striving to redirect our everyday perspectives towards new horizons. *RE-DESIGN: Daily Products of the 21st Century* received both the Icograda Excellence Award and the Icsid Design Excellence Award at the 17th Biennial of Industrial Design and the Mainichi Design Award 2000.

Hara was the lead designer for the Nagano Olympics' opening and closing ceremonies and worked in the promotion of the Aichi EXPO, incorporating into both projects traditional Japanese cultural features. He has been the art director of MUJI since 2002. in addition to designing for a variety of products ranging from sake to coffee, he has worked with the Matsuya Ginza Department Store, the Mori Building, and Tsutaya Books, and was part of the GINZA SIX building renovation. Since 2015, he has been the creative director of "JAPAN HOUSE" sponsored by Japan's Ministry of Foreign Affairs.

His book *Design of Design* (Iwanami Shoten, 2003) received the Suntory Arts and Science Award. After being translated into Mandarin, Korean, and Taiwanese, the book was revised and expanded into an English edition entitled *Designing Design* (Lars Müller Publishers, 2007), reaching global audiences. He has published numerous other books, including *White* (Chuokoron-Shinsha, 2008) and *Designing Japan* (Iwanami Shoten, 2011).

100 WHITES

Author	Kenya Hara

Translator	Josh Trichilo
Translation Editor	Ted Goossen
Proofreader	Sarah Quigley
Editorial Work and Design	
	Kenya Hara + Tomoko Nishi
	Hara Design Institute, Nippon Design Center, Inc.

Publishing	Lars Müller Publishers
	Zurich, Switzerland
	www.lars-mueller-publishers.com

Printing / Binding	Printer Trento, Italy

© 2019/2020 Kenya HARA and Lars Müller Publishers

Printed in Italy

ISBN 978-3-03778-579-9

Distributed in North America by ARTBOOK | D.A.P.
www.artbook.com